ISBN 978-0-259-75972-0
PIBN 10824318

1 MONTH OF
FREE
READING

at
www.ForgottenBooks.com

By purchasing this book you are eligible for one month membership to ForgottenBooks.com, giving you unlimited access to our entire collection of over 1,000,000 titles via our web site and mobile apps.

To claim your free month visit:
www.forgottenbooks.com/free824318

NARRATIVE

OF THE

CAPTIVITY OF MRS. JOHNSON,

CONTAINING

AN ACCOUNT OF HER SUFFERINGS DURING FOUR YEARS WITH THE

INDIANS AND FRENCH.

TOGETHER WITH,

AN APPENDIX,

CONTAINING THE SERMONS PREACHED AT HER FUNERAL, AND THAT OF HER MOTHER, WITH SUNDRY OTHER INTERESTING ARTICLES.

Fourth Edition.

LOWELL:
PUBLISHED BY DANIEL BIXBY,
No. 11 Merrimac Street.
MDCCCXXXIV.

JOHN EMMES DILL, PRINTER,
CORNHILL, BOSTON.

INTRODUCTION.

NOTICES OF THE WILLARD FAMILY.

To trace the progress of families, from their origin to the present day, when perhaps they are spread over the four quarters of the globe, and no memorandums are found, except in the uncertain pages of memory, is a task which can be but feebly performed. In noticing the name of Willard, which was my family name, I cannot pretend to accuracy; but the information which I have collected will perhaps be of some service to others who possess a greater stock. And, if the various branches of families would contribute their mites, it would be an easy way of remedying the deficiency which at present exists in American genealogy.

The first person by the name of Willard, who settled in this country, was Major Willard, whose name is recorded in the History of New England Wars. In the year 1675, in the time of Philip's war—a notorious Indian, who lived within the present limits of the state of Rhode Island—Major Willard, who then lived in the town of Lancaster, in Massachusetts, commanded a troop of horse; and, among his vigorous services, he relieved the town of Brookfield from the Nipnet Indians, who had burnt every house but one, and had almost reduced that to capitulation. When

Lancaster was destroyed by the Indians, Major Willard removed to Salem, where he spent the rest of his days. He had two sons, one of whom was a settled minister in the town of Groton, from which place he was driven by the Indians, and was afterwards installed in Boston. His other son, Simon, established himself on Still River—since taken from Lancaster and incorporated into the town of Harvard. He had nine sons, Simon, Henry, Hezekiah, John, Joseph, Josiah, Samuel, Jonathan, and James. Josiah removed to Winchester, in New Hampshire, and afterwards commanded Fort Dummer. The rest inherited the substance of their father, and lived to very advanced ages in the vicinity of their birth. They all left numerous families, who spread over the United States. His eldest son, Simon, was my grandfather. He had two sons, Aaron and Moses. Aaron lived in Lancaster, and Moses, my father, removed to Lunenburg. I ought to remark, that my grandmother Willard, after the death of her husband, married a person by the name of Farnsworth, by whom she had three sons, who were the first settlers of Charlestown, No. 4. One of them was killed by the Indians.

My father had twelve children. He removed to Charlestown, No. 4, in 1742, and soon had the pleasure to find his children settled around him. He was killed by the Indians, in 1756. My mother died in May, 1797,* and had lived to see

---

* At the age of eighty-four, she busied herself in making a coverlid, which contains something of the remarkable. She did not quite complete it. It now contains upwards of five thousand pieces.

twelve children, ninety-two grandchildren, one hundred and twenty-three great grandchildren, and four great, great grandchildren. The whole that survive are now settled on Connecticut River.

_____

NOTICES OF MR. JAMES JOHNSON.

In the year 1730, my great uncle, Colonel Josiah Willard, while at Boston, was invited to take a walk on the Long Wharf, to view some transports who had just landed from Ireland. A number of gentlemen present were viewing the exercise of some lads, who were placed on shore to exhibit their activity to those who wished to purchase. My uncle spied a boy of some vivacity, of about ten years of age, and who was the only one in the crew who spoke English. He bargained for him. I have never been able to learn the price ; but, as he was afterwards my husband, I am willing to suppose it a considerable sum. ; He questioned the boy about his parentage and descent. All the information he could get, was, that young James, a considerable time previous, went to sea with his uncle, who commanded a ship, and had the appearance of a man of property—that this uncle was taken sick at sea, and died. Immediately after his death, they came in sight of this ship of Irish transports, and he was put on board. His being the only one of the crew who spoke English, and other circumstances, have led his friends to conclude, that this removal on board the Irish ship was done to facilitate the sequestra-

1 †

tion of his uncle's property. He lived with Col.
Willard until he was twenty years old, and then
bought the other year of his time. In 1748, Gov.
Shirley gave him a lieutenant's commission under
Edward Hartwell, Esq.

SITUATION OF THE COUNTRY IN 1744.

It is an old maxim, that, after a man is in possession of a small independent property, it is easy
for him to acquire a great fortune. Just so with
countries; possess them of a few inhabitants, and
let those be unmolested by Indians and enemies,
the land will soon swarm with inhabitants. But
when a feeble band only are gathered together,
and obliged to contend with pestilence, famine,
and the sword, their melancholy numbers will
decrease and waste away. The situation of our
ancestors has often been described, in language
that did honor to the hearts that conceived it.
The boisterous ocean, with unknown shores, hem-
med them in on one side, and a forest, swarming
with savages, yelling for their blood, threatened
on the other. But the same undaunted spirit,
which has defended them in so many perils,
buoyed them above despair, in their early strug-
gles for safety and liberty. I shall be pardoned
the digression, when I observe, that I have, in all
my travels, felt a degree of pride in recollecting
that I belonged to a country whose valor was dis-
tinguished, and whose spirit had never been de-
based by servile submission.

At the age of fourteen, in 1744, I made a visit from Leominster to Charlestown, to visit my parents. Through a long wilderness, from Lunenburg to Lower Ashuelot, now Swanzey, we travelled two days; a solitary house was all the mark of cultivation that occurred on the journey. Guided by marked trees, we travelled cautiously through the gloomy forest, where now the well-tilled farms occupy each rod of ground. From Ashuelot to Charlestown, the passage was opposed, now by 'the Hill of Difficulty,' and now by the Slough Despond. A few solitary inhabitants, who appeared the representatives of wretchedness, were scattered on the way.

When I approached the town of Charlestown, the first object that met my eyes was a party of Indians, holding a war-dance. A cask of rum, which the inhabitants had suffered them to partake of, had raised their spirits to all the horrid yells and feats of distortion which characterize the nation. I was chilled at the sight, and passed tremblingly by. At this time, Charlestown contained nine or ten families, who lived in huts not far distant from each other. The Indians were numerous, and sssociated in a friendly manner with the whites. It was the most northerly settlement on Connecticut River, and the adjacent country was terribly wild. A saw-mill was erected, and the first boards were sawed while I was there. The inhabitants commemorated the event with a dance, which took place on new boards. In those days there was such a mixture on the frontiers, of savages and settlers, without established laws to govern them, that the state of society cannot easily be described; and the impending dangers of war, where-it was known that the savages would join the enemies of our country, retarded the progress of refinement and cultivation. The inhabitants of Charlestown began to erect a fort, and took some steps towards clearing their farms; but war soon checked their industry.

CHARLESTOWN.

In the year 1740, the first settlement was made in the town of Charlestown, then known by the name of No. 4, by three families, who emigrated from Lunenburg, by the name of Farnsworth. That part of New Hampshire west of Merrimac River was then a trackless wilderness. Within a few years past, instances have been known of new townships, totally uninhabited, becoming thick-settled villages in the course of six or seven years. But in those days, when government was weak—when savages were on our borders, and Frenchmen in Canada—population extended with timorous and tardy paces; in the course of twelve years, the families increased only to twenty-two or three. The human race will not flourish unless fostered by the warm sunshine of peace.

During the first twenty years of its existence as a settled place, until the peace between Great Britain and France, it suffered all the consternation and ravages of war; not that warfare which civilized nations wage with each other, but the cruel carnage of savages and Frenchmen. Sometimes engaged in the duties of the camp, at others sequestering themselves from surrounding enemies, they became familiar with danger, but not with industrious husbandry.

In the year 1744, the inhabitants began to erect a fort for their safety. When the Cape Breton war commenced, the Indians assumed the hatchet, and began their depredations on Charlestown on the 19th day of April, A.D., 1746, by burning the mills, and taking Capt. John Spafford, Isaac Parker, and Stephen Farnsworth, prisoners. On the second day of May following, Seth Putnam was killed. Two days after, Capt. Payne arrived with a troop of horse from Massachusetts, to defend the place. About twenty of his men had the curiosity to view the place where Putnam was killed, and were ambushed by the Indians. Capt. Stevens, who commanded a few men, rushed out of the fort to their relief; a sharp combat ensued, in which the Indians were routed. They left some guns and blankets on the field of action, but they carried their dead off with them, which is a policy they never omit. Ensign Obadiah Sartwell was captured, and Samuel Farnsworth, Elijah Allen, Peter Perrin, Aaron Lyon, aud Josep Massey, fell victims to Indian vengeance. h

On the 19th of June, a severe engagement took place. Capt. Brown, from Stow, in Massachusetts, had previously arrived with some troops. A party of his joined a number of Capt. Stevens's soldiers, to go into the meadow after their horses. The dogs discovered an ambush, which put them into a posture for action, and gave them the advantage of the first fire. This disconcerted the savages, who, being on higher ground, overshot, and did but little damage to the English. The enemy were routed, and even seen to drag several dead bodies after them. They left behind them guns, spears, and blankets, which sold at 40l., old tenor. During the time Capt. Josiah Brown assisted in defending the fort, Jedediah Winchel was killed, and Samuel Stanhope, Coronet Baker, and David Parker, were wounded. During this summer, the fort was entirely blockaded, and all were obliged to take refuge within the piquets. On the 3d day of August, one Phillips was killed, within a few feet of the fort, as he accidentally stepped out; at night, a soldier crept to him with a rope, and he was drawn into the fort and interred. In the summer of the year 1746, Capt. Ephraim Brown, from Sudbury, arrived with a troop of horse, to relieve Capt. Josiah Brown. The Sudbury troop tarried about a month, and were relieved by a company commanded by Capt. Winchester, who defended the place till autumn, when the inhabitants, fatigued with watching, and weary of the dangers of the forest, deserted the place entirely for about six months. In the month of August, previous to the evacuation, the Indians, assisted by their brethren the French, were very troublesome and mischievous; they destroyed all the horses, hogs, and cattle. An attack was made on the fort, which lasted two days. My father at this time lost ten cattle; but the people were secured behind their wooden walls, and received but little damage.

In this recess of the settlement of No. 4, the Indians and French were ice-locked in Canada, and the frontiers suffered only in apprehension. In March, 1747, Capt. Phinehas Stevens, who commanded a ranging party of about 30 men, marched to No. 4, and took possession of the fort. He found it uninjured by the enemy, and an old spaniel and a cat, who had been domesticated before the evacuation, had guarded it safely through the winter, and gave the troops a hearty welcome to their tenement.

Capt. Stevens was of eminent service to the infant settlement. In 1748, he moved his family to the place, and encouraged the settlers by his fortitude and industry. In the early part of his life, when Rutland suffered by savage vengeance, when the Rev. Mr. Willard was murdered, he was taken prisoner, and carried to St. Francis. This informed him of the Indian customs, and familiarized him with their mode of warfare. He was an active, penetrating soldier, and a respectable, worthy citizen.

In a few days after the fort was taken possession of by Capt. Stevens's troops, a party of 500 French and Indians, commanded by Mons. Debelcie, sallied from their den in Canada, and made a furious attack on the fort. The battle lasted five days, and every stratagem, which French policy or Indian malice could invent, was practised to reduce the garison. Sometimes they made an onset by a discharge of musquetry ; at others, they discharged fire-arrows, which communicated fire to several parts of the fort. But these were insufficient to daunt the courage of the little band that were assailed. Their next step was to fill a cart with combustibles, and roll it against the walls, to communicate fire; but the English kept up such a brisk, incessant fire, that they were defeated in the project. At length the monsieurs, tired with fighting, beat a parley; two Indians, formerly acquainted with Capt. Stevens, came as negociators, and wished to exchange some furs for corn; this Capt. Stevens refused, but offered a bushel of corn for each hostage they would leave, to be exchanged at some future day. These terms were not complied with; and on the fifth day the enemy retreated, at which time the soldiers at the garrison honored them with as brisk a discharge as they could afford, to let them know they were neither disheartened, nor exhausted in ammunition. The garrison had none killed; and only one, by the name of Brown, was wounded.

Perhaps no place was ever defended with greater bravery than this fort, during this action: 30 or 40 men, when attacked by 500, must have an uncommon degree of fortitude and vigilance, to defend themselves during five days. But Capt. Stevens was equal to the task, and will be applauded by posterity. After the battle, he sent an express to Boston with the tidings. Gov. Charles Knowles happened to be then at Boston, and rewarded Capt. Stevens with a handsome sword—in gratitude for which, the place was afterwards called Charlestown.

In November, 1747, a body of the troops set out from the fort, to return to Massachusetts. They had not proceeded far, before the Indians fired on them. Isaac Goodale and Nathaniel Gould were killed; and one Anderson taken prisoner. From this period until the end of the Cape

Breton war, the fort was defended by Capt. Stevens. Soldiers passed and repassed to Canada, but the inhabitants took sanctuary in the fort, and made but little progress in cultivation. During the Indian wars, which lasted till the year 1760, Charlestown was noted more for its feats of war, than a place of rapid improvement. Settlers thought it more prudent to remain with their friends in safety, than risk their scalps with savage power. Since that period, it has become a flourishing village, and contains all that a rural situation affords of the useful and pleasant. Numerous farms and stately buildings now flourish where the savage roamed the forest. The prosperity of the town was greatly promoted by the Rev. Mr. Bulkely Olcott, who was a settled minister there about 32 years. In the character of this good man was combined the agreeable companion, the industrious citizen, and unaffected Christian. During the whole of his ministry, his solicitude for the happiness of his parishoners was as conspicuous in the benefits they received from his assistance, as in their sincere attachment to his person. As a divine, he was pathetic, devout, and instructive, and may with propriety be said to have

Shown the path to Heaven, and led the way.

He was highly respected through life. In June, 1793, he died, much lamented.

REMOVAL TO CHARLESTOWN.

In May, 1749, we received information of the cessation of arms between Great Britain and France. I had then been married about two years, and Mr. Johnson's enterprising spirit was zealous to remove to Charlestown. In June we undertook the hazardous and fatiguing journey ; we arrived safe at the fort, and found five families, who had ventured so far into the woods during hostilities. But the gloomy forest, and warlike appearance of the place, soon made me homesick. Two or three days after my arrival, orders came from Massachusetts to withdraw the troops. Government placed confidence in the proffered peace of Frenchmen, and withdrew even the appearance of hostility. But French treachery and savage malice will ever keep pace with each other. Without even the suspicion of danger, the inhabitants went about their business of husbandry. The day the soldiers left the fort, Ensign Obadiah Sartwell went to harrow some corn, and took Enos Stevens, the fourth son of Phinehas Stevens, Esq., to ride the horse. My father and two brothers were at work in the meadow. Early in the afternoon, the Indians appeared, and shot Ensign Sartwell and the horse, and took young Stevens prisoner. In addition to this, my father and brothers were in the meadow, and we supposed they must be destroyed. My husband was gone to Northfield. In the fort were seven women and four men. The anxiety and grief we experienced was the highest imaginable. The next night we despatched a post to Boston, to carry the news of our disaster; but my father and brothers did not return. The next day but one, my husband and five or six others arrived from Northfield. We kept close in the garrison, suffering every apprehension, for ten or twelve days, when the sentry from the box cried out that troops were coming. Joyful at the relief, we all mounted on the top of the fort, and among the rest discovered my father. He, on hearing the guns, supposed the fort was destroyed, left his team in the meadow, and made the best of his way to Northfield with my two brothers. The soldiers were about thirty in number, and headed by Major Josiah Willard, of Fort Dummer. Enos Stevens was carried to Montreal, but the French commander sent him back directly, by the way of Albany. This was the last damage done the frontiers during the Cape Breton war.

CURSORY NOTICES.

A DETAIL of the miseries of a 'frontier man' must excite the pity of every child of humanity. The gloominess of the rude forest, the distance from friends and competent defence, and the daily him company; at home, the distresses of a wife, and the tears of lisping children, often unman the soul that real danger assailed in vain. Those who can recollect the war that existed between France and England, fifty years ago, may figure to themselves the unhappy situation of the inhabitants on the frontiers of New Hampshire. The malice of the French in Canada, and the exasperated savages that dwelt in their vicinity, rendered the tedious days and frightful nights a season of unequalled calamities. The daily reports of captured families and slaughtered friends mingled grief with fear. Had there been an organized government, to stretch forth its protecting arm in any case of danger, the misery might have been in a degree alleviated. But the infancy of our country did not admit of this blessing. While Gov. Shirley, of Massachusetts, was petitioning to England for a fleet and army, Benning Wentworth, the governor of New Hampshire, implicitly obeying the advice of his friend Shirley, remained inactively secure at his seat at Portsmouth. At the commencement of the year 1745, the expedition to Louisburg was projected, the success of which originated from the merest accident, rather than from military valor or generalship: this drained New Hampshire of most of its effective men. From this period till the peace, which took place in the year 1749, the savages committed frequent depredations on the defenceless inhabitants; and the ease with which they gained their prey encouraged their boldness, and, by scattering in small parties, they were able to infest the whole frontier of New Hampshire, from Fort Dummer, on Connecticut River, to the lowest settlement on Merrimac. During this war, which is known by the name of the Cape Breton war, the town of No. 4 could hardly be said to be inhabited; some adventurers had made a beginning, but few were considered as belonging to the town. Capt. Stevens, whose valor is recorded as an instance of consummate generalship, part of the time kept the fort, which afforded a shelter to the enterprising settlers, in times of imminent danger. But even his vigilance did not save the town from numerous scenes of carnage. At the commencement of the peace, in 1749, the enterprising spirit of New England rose superior to the dangers of the forest, and they began to venture innovation. The Indians, still thirsty for plunder and rapine, and regardless of the peace which their masters, the French, had concluded, kept up a flying warfare, and committed several outrages upon life and property; this kept the increasing inhabitants in a state of alarm for three or four years; most of the time they performed their daily work without molestation, but retreated to the fort on each returning night.

Our country has so long been exposed to Indian wars, that recitals of exploits and sufferings, of escapes and deliverances, have become both numerous and trite. The air of novelty will not be attempted in the following pages; simple facts, unadorned, is what the reader must expect; pity for my sufferings, and admiration at my safe return, is all that my history can excite. The aged man, while perusing, will probably turn his attention to the period when the facts took place; his memory will be refreshed with the sad tidings of his country's sufferings, which gave a daily wound to his feelings, between the years 1740 and 1760. By contrasting those days with the present, he may rejoice that he witnesses those times which many have 'waited for, but died without a sight.' Those in early life, while they commisserate the sufferings which their parents and ancestors endured, may felicitate themselves, that their lines fell in a land of peace, where neither savages nor neighboring wars molest their happiness.

NARRATIVE.

CHAPTER I.

Situation until August 31, 1754.

SOME of the soldiers who arrived with Major Willard, with the inhabitants who bore arms, were commanded by Capt. Stevens the rest of the year 1749, and part of the following spring; after which, the inhabitants resided pretty much in the fort, until the spring or fall of the year 1752. They cultivated their lands in some degree, but they put but little confidence in the savages.

The continuation of peace began by degrees to appease the resentment of the Indians; and they appeared to discover a wish for friendly intercourse. The inhabitants in No. 4 and its vicinity

blankets and other necessaries, and in most instances they were punctual in payment. During
the year 1753, all was harmony and safety. Settlements increased with tolerable rapidity, and
the new country began to assume the appearance
of cultivation.

The commencement of the year 1754 began to
threaten another rupture between the French and
English; and, as the dividing line between Canada
and the English colonies was the object of con-
tention, it was readily seen, that the frontier
towns would be in imminent danger. But, as
immediate war was not expected, Mr. Johnson
thought that he might risk the safety of his family,
while he made a tour to Connecticut, for trade.
He sat out the last of May, and his absence of
three months was a tedious season to me. Soon
after his departure, every body was 'tremblingly
alive' with fear. The Indians were reported to
be on their march for our destruction, and our
distance from sources of information gave full
latitude for exaggeration of news, before it reached our ears. The fears of the night were borri-
ble beyond description, and even the light of day
was far from dispelling painful anxiety. While
looking from the windows of my log-house, and
seeing my neighbors tread cautiously by each
hedge and hillock, lest some secreted savage
might start forth to take their scalp, my fears
would baffle description. Alarms grew louder and
louder, till our apprehensions were too strongly
confirmed, by the news of the capture of Mr. Ma-
loon's family, on Merrimac River; this reached us
about the 20th of August. Imagination now saw

and heard a thousand Indians; and I never went round my own house, without first looking with trembling caution by each corner, to see if a tomahawk was not raised for my destruction.

On the 24th of August, I was relieved from all my fears, by the arrival of my husband. He brought intelligence from Connecticut, that a war was expected the next spring, but that no immediate danger was contemplated. He had made preparations to remove to Northfield, as soon as our stock of hay was consumed, and our dozen of swine had demolished our ample stores of grain, which would secure his family and property from the miseries and ravages of war. Our eldest son, Sylvanus, who was six years old, was in the mean time to be put to school at Springfield. Mr. Johnson brought home a large addition to his stores, and the neighbors made frequent parties at our house, to express their joy for his return, and time passed merrily off, by the aid of spirit and a ripe yard of melons. As I was in the last days of pregnancy, I could not join so heartily in their good cheer as I otherwise might. Yet, in a new country, pleasure is often derived from sources unknown to those less accustomed to the woods. The return of my husband, the relief from danger, the crowds of happy friends, combined to render my situation peculiarly agreeable. I now boasted with exultation, that I should, with husband, friends, and luxuries, live happy, in spite of the fear of savages.

On the evening of the 29th of August, our house was visited by a party of neighbors, who spent the time very cheerfully, with watermelons and flip, till midnight; they all then retired in

high spirits, except a spruce young spark, who
tarried a few hours longer, to keep company with
my sister. Unsuspicious of danger, we went to
bed with feelings well tuned for sleep. But O the
transition in the morning! Well would it have
been for us, if we had observed the caution of the
poet :—

' But farewell now to unsuspicious nights,
And slumbers unalarmed! Now, ere you sleep,
See that your polished arms are primed with care,
And drop the night-bolt :—ruffians are abroad ;
And the first larum of the cock's shrill throat
May prove a trumpet, summoning your ear
To horrid sounds of hostile feet within.
E'en day-light has its dangers ; and the walk
Through pathless wastes and woods, unconscious once
Of other tenants than melodious birds,
Or harmless flocks, is hazardous and bold.' cowper.

We rested with fine composure, till midway
between daybreak and sunrise, when we were
roused by neighbor Labarree's knocking at the
door, who had shouldered his axe to a day's work
for my husband. Mr. Johnson slipped on his
jacket and trowsers, and stepped to the door to
let him in. But by opening the door he opened a
scene terrible to describe. Indians! Indians!
were the first words I heard. He sprang to his
guns, but Labarree, heedless of danger, instead of
closing the door to keep them out, began to rally
our hired men up stairs, for not rising earlier; but
in an instant a crowd of savages, fixed horribly for
war, rushed furiously in. I screamed, and begged my friends to ask for quarter. By this time
they were all over the house; some up stairs,
hauling my sister out of bed ; another had hold of
me, and one was approaching Mr. Johnson, who
stood in the middle of the floor to deliver himself

up ; but the Indian, supposing that he would make resistance, and be more than his match, went to the door and brought three of his comrades, and the four bound him. I was led to the door, fainting and trembling ; there stood my friend Labarree, bound ; Ebenezer Farnsworth, whom they found up chamber, they were putting in the same situation ; and, to complete the shocking scene, my three little children were driven naked to the place where I stood. On viewing myself, I found that I too was naked. An Indian had plundered three gowns, who, on seeing my situation, gave me the whole. I asked another for a petticoat, but he refused it. After what little plunder their hurry would allow them to get was confusedly bundled up, we were ordered to march. After going about 20 rods, we fell behind a rising ground, where we halted, to pack the things in a better manner ; while there, a savage went back, as we supposed, to fire the buildings. Farnsworth proposed to my husband to go back with him, to get a quantity of pork from the cellar, to help us on our journey ; but Mr. Johnson prudently replied, that by that means the Indians might find the rum, and in a fit of intoxication kill us all. The Indian presently returned with marks of fear in his countenance,* and we were hurried on with all violence. Two savages laid hold of each of my

* This, as we afterwards found, was occasioned by his meeting Mr. Osmer at the door of the house, who lodged in the chamber, and had secreted himself behind a box, and was then making his escape. He run directly to the fort, and the alarm guns were fired. My father, Mr. Moses Willard, was then second in command. Capt. Stevens was for sallying out with a party for our relief ; but my father begged him to desist, as the Indians made it an invariable practice to kill their prisoners when attacked.

arms, and hurried me through thorny thickets in a most unmerciful manner. I lost a shoe, and suffered exceedingly. We heard the alarm guns from the fort. This added new speed to the flight of the savages. They were apprehensive that soldiers might be sent for our relief. When we had got a mile and a half, my faintness obliged me to sit. This being observed by an Indian, he drew his knife, as I supposed, to put an end to my existence. But he only cut some bands with which my gown was tied, and then pushed me on. My little children were crying, my husband and the other two men were bound, and my sister and myself were obliged to make the best of our way, with all our might. The loss of my shoe rendered travelling extremely painful. At the distance of three miles, there was a general halt; the savages, supposing that we, as well as themselves, might have an appetite for breakfast, gave us a loaf of bread, some raisins, and apples, which they had taken from the house. While we were forcing down our scanty breakfast, a horse came in sight, known to us all by the name of Scoggin, belonging to Phinehas Stevens, Esq. One of the Indians attempted to shoot him, but was prevented by Mr. Johnson. They then expressed a wish to catch him, saying, by pointing to me, for squaw to ride : my husband had previously been unbound, to assist the children ; he, with two Indians, caught the horse on the banks of the river. By this time, my legs and feet were covered with blood, which being noticed by Mr. Labarree, he, with that humanity which never forsook him, took his own stockings and presented them to me, and the Indians gave me a pair of moggasons. Bags and blankets were thrown over Scoggin, and I mounted on the top of them, and on we jogged about seven miles, to the upper end of Wilcott's Island. We there halted, and prepared to cross the river. Rafts were made of dry timber; two Indians and Farnsworth crossed first; Labarree, by signs, got permission to swim the horse, and Mr. Johnson was allowed to swim by the raft that I was on, to push it along. We all arrived safe on the other side of the river, about four o'clock in the afternoon; a fire was kindled, and some of their stolen kettles were hung over it, and filled with porridge. The savages took delight in viewing their spoil, which amounted to forty or fifty pounds in value. They then, with a true savage yell, gave the war-whoop, and bid defiance to danger. As our tarry in this place lasted an hour, I had time to reflect on our miserable situation. Captives in the power of unmerciful savages, without provision, and almost without clothes, in a wilderness where we must sojourn as long as the children of Israel did, for aught we knew, and, what added to our distress, not one of our savage masters could understand a word of English. Here, after being hurried from home with such rapidity, I have leisure to inform the reader respecting our Indian masters. They were eleven* in number, men of middle age, except one, a youth of sixteen, who, in our journey, discovered a very mischievous and troublesome disposition. According to their national practice, he who first laid hands on a

---

* Mr. Labarree is very positive, and I think Mr. Johnson was of the same opinion, that seventeen Indians attacked the house; the other six might have been a scouting party, that watched till we were out of danger, and then took another route.

prisoner considered him as his property. My
master, who was the one that took my hand when
I sat on the bed, was as clever an Indian as ever
I saw; he even evinced, at numerous times, a
disposition that showed he was by no means void
of compassion. The four who took my husband
claimed him as their property, and my sister,
three children, Labarree, and Farnsworth, had
each a master. When the time came for us to
prepare to march, I almost expired at the thought
—to leave my aged parents, brothers, sisters, and
friends, and travel with savages, through a dismal
forest to unknown regions, in the alarming situation I then was in, with three small children.
The eldest, Sylvanus, who was but six years old.
My eldest daughter, Susanna, was four, and Polly,
the other, two. My sister Miriam was fourteen.
My husband was barefoot, and otherwise thinly
clothed; his master had taken his jacket, and
nothing but his shirt and trowsers remained. My
two daughters had nothing but their shifts, and I
only the gown that was handed me by the savages.
In addition to the sufferings which arose from my
own deplorable condition, I could not but feel
for my friend Labarree; he had left a wife and
four small children behind, to lament his loss,
and to render his situation extremely unhappy.
With all these misfortunes lying heavily upon me,
the reader can imagine my situation. The Indians pronounced the dreadful word, 'Munch,'
march, and on we must go. I was put on the
horse; Mr. Johnson took one daughter, and Mr.
Labarree, being unbound, took the other. We
went six or eight miles, and stopped for the night.
The men were made secure, by having their legs

put in split sticks, somewhat like stocks, and tied
with cords, which were tied to the limbs of trees
too high to be reached. My sister, much to her
mortification, must lie between two Indians, with
a cord thrown over her, and passing under each
of them; the little children had blankets, and I
was allowed one for my use. Thus we took
lodging for the night, with the sky for a covering,
and the ground for a pillow. The fatigues of the
preceeding day obliged me to sleep several hours,
in spite of the horrors which surrounded me. The
Indians observed great silence, and never spoke
but when really necessary, and all the prisoners
were disposed to say but little. My children were
much more peaceable than could be imagined:
gloomy fear imposed a deadly silence.

CHAPTER II.

*History of our Journey through the Wilderness, till
we came to the Waters that enter Lake Champlain.*

In the morning we were roused before sunrise.
The Indians struck up a fire, hung on their stolen
kettles, and made us some watergruel for breakfast. After a few sips of this meagre fare, I was
again put on the horse, with my husband by my
side, to hold me on. My two fellow-prisoners
took the little girls, and we marched sorrowfully
on for an hour or two, when a keener distress was
added to my multiplied afflictions: I was taken
with the pangs of childbirth. The Indians signified to us that we must go on to a brook. When

we got there, they showed some humanity, by making a booth for me. Here the compassionate reader will drop a fresh tear for my inexpressible distress: fifteen or twenty miles from the abode of any civilized being, in the open wilderness, rendered cold by a rainy day, in one of the most perilous hours, and unsupplied with the least necessary, that could yield convenience in this hazardous moment. My children were crying at a distance, where they were held by their masters, and only my husband and sister to attend me. None but mothers can figure to themselves my unhappy fortune. The Indians kept aloof the whole time. About ten o'clock a daughter was born.* They then brought me some articles of

* In September, 1797, I made a tour, accompanied by Elijah Grout, Esq., and my daughter, E. C. Kimball, to Weathersfield, to find the spot of ground where my daughter was born, but could not find it to my satisfaction at that time. In August, 1790, I again set off for the same purpose, accompanied by my daughter aforesaid, and was joined by Nathaniel Stoton, Esq., and Mrs. Whipple, of Weathersfield. In this tour we passed two small streams, and, on coming to the third, I was convinced it must be up that stream some small distance. I requested a halt, and, on viewing a cliff of rocks, I informed my company that we were not far from the place. The reader may well suppose, that I was not a little overjoyed at the expectation of viewing the place where I had undergone so much sorrow. The keenest anguish of soul, the providential deliverance, and the almost miraculous preservation, has ever rendered the recollection of that spot dear to me, and it can only be forgotten with my existence. We pursued up the stream a little farther, and, on viewing the rocks aforesaid, I knew them to be the same which were spoken of by my husband and others, on the morning of our departure on our journey with the Indians, which rock, they said, would remain as a monument, that, should any of us ever be so happy as to return, we might find the place, although at that time it was nothing but a wilderness. We also discovered a bog-meadow, where the horse mired with me, in the morning prior to the birth of my child. And I recollected that it was nigh the brook, or when crossing the stream, that I felt the

clothing for the child, which they had taken from the house. My master looked into the booth, and clapped his hands with joy, crying, 'Two monies for me, two monies for me.' I was permitted to rest the remainder of the day. The Indians were employed in making a bier for the prisoners to carry me on, and another booth for my lodging during night. They brought a needle and two pins, and some bark to tie the child's clothes, which they gave my sister, and a large wooden spoon to feed it with; at dusk they made some porridge, and brought a cup to steep some roots in, which Mr. Labarree had provided. In the evening I was removed to the new booth. For supper, they made more porridge, and some

first pangs which were indicative of the sorrowful scene that soon followed. And, from the rocks before mentioned, the bog-meadows, the stream, and a dry spot of ground, resembling the one on which the savages built my booth—circumstances that could not well be forgotten—I was very well satisfied, as to its being the place for which I had sought. However, that I might be still more certain—as I purposed to have a monument erected on the spot—in 1799, I again set out, accompanied by my friend and fellow-prisoner, Mr. Labarree, and took a further view, to ascertain with more precision the memorable place. When we had arrived, we were both agreed as to the identical spot of ground, even within a few feet, and ascertained that it was on the northeast corner lot of land in Cavendish, and is about half a mile from the main road leading from Weathersfield to Reading, where is erected a monument, with the following inscription, which the friendly reader may peruse, if he should ever pass that way :—

'This is near the spot where the Indians encamped, the night after they took Mr. Johnson and family, Mr. Labarree, and Farnsworth, August 30, 1754; and Mrs. Johnson was delivered of her child, half a mile up this brook.

'When trouble's near the Lord is kind;
    He hears the captive's cry :
 He can subdue the savage mind,
    And learn it sympathy.'

johnny-cakes. My portion was brought me in a little bark. I slept that night far beyond expectation.

In the morning we were summoned for the journey, after the usual breakfast of meal and water. I, with my infant in my arms, was laid on the litter, which was supported alternately by Mr. Johnson, Labarree, and Farnsworth. My sister and son were put upon Scoggin, and the two little girls rode on their master's backs. Thus we proceeded two miles, when my carriers grew too faint to proceed any further. This being observed by our sable masters, a general halt was called, and they embodied themselves for council. My master soon made signs to Mr. Johnson, that, if I could ride on the horse, I might proceed; otherwise, I must be left behind. Here I observed marks of pity in his countenance; but this might arise from the fear of losing his two monies. I preferred an

Another monument is erected on the spot of ground where the child was born, with this inscription:—

'On the 31st of August, A.D., 1754, Capt. James Johnson had a daughter born on this spot of ground—being captivated with his whole family, by the Indians.

'If mothers e'er should wander here,
They'll drop a sympathetic tear
For her, who, in the howling wild
Was safe delivered of a child.'

In June, 1808, I for the last time visited the place, where, almost fifty-four years before, I had experienced the keenest sorrow that perhaps was ever equalled by any woman. I was accompanied by Col. Kimball and my daughter, E. Captive, his wife, to Weathersfield, and there we were joined by Capt. Sherwin and his wife, and Mr. Demell Grout.—This Mr. Demell Grout was a son of Mrs. Grout, who was in captivity at the same time that I was; and his given name was to keep in remembrance the name of the gentleman who bought his mother from the Ir attempt to ride on the horse, rather than to perish miserably alone. Mr. Labarree took the infant, and every step of the horse almost deprived me of life. My weak and helpless condition rendered me, in a degree, insensible to every thing. My poor child could have no sustenance from my breast, and was supported entirely by watergruel. My other little children, rendered peevish by an uneasy mode of riding, often burst into cries, but a surly check from their masters soon silenced them. We proceeded on with a slow, mournful pace. My weakness was too severe to allow me to sit on the horse long at a time; every hour I was taken off, and laid on the ground to rest. This preserved my life during the third day. At night we found ourselves at the head of Black River Pond. Here we prepared to spend the night. Our supper consisted of gruel, and the broth of a hawk they had killed the preceeding day. The prisoners were secured, as usual; a booth was made for me, and all went to rest. After encamp. ment, we entered into a short conversation. My sister observed, that, if I could have been left behind, our trouble would have been seemingly nothing. My husband hoped, by the assistance of Providence, we should all be preserved. Mr. Labarree pitied his poor family, and Farnsworth summed the whole of his wishes, by saying that, if he could have got a layer of pork from the cellar, we should not be in fear of starvation. The night was uncommonly dark, and passed tediously off.

In the morning, half chilled with a cold fog, we were ordered from our places of rest, offered the lean fare of meal and water, and then prepared for the journey. Every thing resembled a funeral procession. The savages preserved their gloomy sadness; the prisoners, bowed down with grief and fatigue, felt little disposition to talk; and the unevenness of the country, sometimes lying in miry plains, at others rising into steep and broken hills, rendered our passage hazardous and painful. Mr. Labarree kept the infant in his arms, and preserved its life. The fifth day's journey was an unvaried scene of fatigue. The Indians sent out two or three hunting parties, who returned without game. As we had in the morning consumed the last morsel of our meal, every one now began to be seriously alarmed, and hunger, with all its horrors, looked us earnestly in the face. At night, we found the waters that run into Lake Champlain, which was over the height of land; before dark, we halted, and the Indians, by the help of their punk, which they carried in horns, made a fire. They soon adopted a plan to relieve their hunger. The horse was shot, and his flesh was in a few moments broiled on embers, and they, with native gluttony, satiated their craving appetites. To use the term politeness, in the management of their repast, may be thought a burlesque; yet their offering the prisoners the best parts of the horse certainly bordered on civility; an epicure could not have catered nicer slices, nor, in that situation, served them up with more neatness. Appetite is said to be the best sauce; yet our abundance of it did not render savory this novel steak. My children, however, eat too much, which made them very unwell for a number of days. Broth was made for me and my child, which was rendered almost a luxury by the seasoning of roots. After supper, countenances began to brighten; those who had relished the meal, exhibited new strength, and those who had only snuffed its effluvia, confessed themselves regaled; the evening was employed in drying and smoking what remained for future use. The night was a scene of distressing fears to me, and my extreme weakness, had affected my mind to such a degree, that every difficulty appeared doubly terrible. By the assistence of Scoggin, I had been brought so far; yet, so great was my debility, that every hour I was taken off and laid on the ground, to keep me from expiring. But now, alas! this conveyance was no more. To walk was impossible. Inevitable death in the midst of woods, one hundred miles wide, appeared my only portion.

CHAPTER III.

Continuation till our arrival at East Bay, in Lake Champlain.

IN the morning of the sixth day, the Indians exerted themselves to prepare one of their greatest dainties. The marrowbones of old Scoggin were pounded for a soup, and every root, both sweet and bitter, that the woods afforded, was thrown in, to give it a flavor. Each one partook of as much as his feelings would allow. The warwhoop then resounded, with an infernal yell, and we began to fix for a march. My fate was unknown, till my master brought some bark, and tied my petticoats as high as he supposed would be convenient for walking, and ordered me to 'Munch.' With scarce strength to stand alone, I went on half a mile, with my little son and three Indians. The rest were advanced. My power to move then failed; the world grew dark, and I dropped down. I had sight enough to see an Indian lift his hatchet over my head, while my little son screamed, ' Ma'am, do go, for they will kill you.' As I fainted, my last thought was, that I should presently be in the world of spirits. When I awoke, my master was talking angrily with the savage who had threatened my life. By his gestures, I could learn, that he charged him with not acting the honorable part of a warrior, by an attempt to destroy the prize of a brother. A whoop was given for a halt. My master helped me to the rest of the company, where a council was held, the result of which was, that my husband should walk by my side, and help me along. This he did for some hours, but faintness then overpowered me, and Mr. Johnson's tenderness and solicitude was unequal to the task of aiding me further. Another council was held: while in debate, as I lay on the ground, gasping for breath, my master sprang towards me with his hatchet. My husband and fellow-prisoners grew pale at the sight, suspecting that he, by a single blow, would rid themselves of so. great a burthen as I was. But he had yet too much esteem for his 'two monies.' His object was to get bark from a tree, to make a packsaddle, for my conveyance on the back of my husband. He took me up, and we marched in that form the rest of the day. Mr. Labarree still kept my infant, Farnsworth carried one of the little. girls, and the other. rode with her master. They were extremely sick and weak, owing to the large portion of the horse which they eat; but if they-uttered a murmuring word, a menacing frown from the savages soon imposed silence. None of the Indians were disposed to show insults of any nature, except the youngest, which I have before mentioned. He often delighted himself by tormenting my sister, by pulling her hair, treading on her gown, and numerous other boyish pranks, which were provoking and troublesome. We moved on, faint and wearily, till night; the Indians then yelled their war-whoop, built a fire, and hung over their horse-broth. After supper, my booth was built, as usual, and I reposed much better than I had the preceeding nights.

In the morning, I found myself greatly restored. Without the aid of physicians or physic, nature had began the cure of that weakness to which she

had reduced me but a few days before. The
reader will be tired of the repetition of the same
materials for our meals; but if my feelings can be
realized, no one will turn with disgust from a
breakfast of steaks, which were cut from the thigh
of a horse. After which, Mr. Johnson was ordered
to take the infant, and go forward with part of
the company. I 'munched' in the rear till we
came to a beaver-pond, which was formed in a
branch of Otter Creek. Here I was obliged to
wade; when half way over, up to the middle in
cold water, my little strength failed, and my
power to speak or see left me. While motionless
and stiffened in the middle of the pond, I was
perceived from the other side, by Mr. Johnson,
who laid down the infant, and came to my assistance; he took me in his arms, and, when the
opposite side was gained, life itself had apparently forsaken me. The whole company stopped,
and the Indians, with more humanity than I supposed them possessed of, busied themselves in
making a fire, to warm me into life. The warm
influence of the fire restored my exhausted strength
by degrees, and in two hours I was told to ' Munch.'
The rest of the day I was carried by my husband.
In the middle of the afternoon, we arrived on the
banks of one of the great branches of Otter Creek.
Here we halted, and two savages, who had been
on a hunting scout, returned with a duck; a fire
was made, which was thrice grateful to my cold,
shivering limbs. Six days had now almost elapsed,
since the fatal morn in which we were taken, and,
by the blessing of that Providence, whose smiles
give life to creation, we were still in existence.
My wearied husband, naked children, and help-

less infant, formed a scene that conveyed severer pangs to my heart, than all the sufferings I endured myself. The Indians were sullen and silent, the prisoners were swollen with gloomy grief, and I was half the time expiring. After my feelings were a little quickened by warmth, my sad portion was brought in a bark, consisting of the duck's head, and a gill of broth. As I lifted the unsavory morsel, with a trembling hand, to my mouth, I cast my thoughts back a few days, to a time when, from a board plentifully spread, in my own house, I eat my food with a merry heart. The wooden spoon dropped from my feeble hand. The contrast was too affecting. Seated on a ragged rock, beneath a hemlock, as I then was—emaciated by sickness, and surrounded by my weeping and distressed family, who were helpless prisoners—despair would have robbed me of life, had I not put my whole confidence in that Being who has power to save. Our masters began to prepare to ford the stream. I swallowed most of my broth, and was taken up by my husband. The river was very rapid, and passing dangerous. Mr. Labarree, when half over with my child, was tripped up by its rapidity, and lost the babe in the water. Little did I expect to see the poor thing again; but he fortunately reached a corner of its blanket, and saved its life. The rest got safe to the other shore. Another fire was built, and my sister dried the infant and its clothes.

Here we found a proof of Indian sagacity, which might justly be supposed not to belong to a band of rambling barbarians. In their journey over to the Connecticut River, they had, in this place, killed a bear. The entrails were cleansed, and

filled with the fat of the animal, and suspended
from the limb of a tree ; by it was deposited a bag
of flour, and some tobacco, all which was designed for future stores, when travelling that way.
Nothing could have been offered more acceptable
than these tokens of Indian economy and pru-
dence. The flour was made into pudding, and
the bear-grease sauce was not unrelishing. Broth
was made, and well seasoned with snakeroot, and
those who were fond of tobacco had each their
share. The whole formed quite a sumptuous en-
tertainment. But these savage dainties made no
sensible addition to our quota of happiness. My
weakness increased, my children were very unwell, and Mr. Johnson's situation was truly distressing. By travelling barefoot over such a
length of forest, and supporting me on his shoulders, his feet were rendered sore beyond description. I cannot express too much gratitude for Mr.
Labarree's goodness. My infant was his sole
charge, and he supported it by pieces of the horse-
flesh, which he kept for its use, which, by being
first chewed in his own mouth, and then put into
the child's, afforded it the necessary nutriment.
After supper, my booth was made, the evening
yell was sounded, and we encamped for the night.
By this time the savages had relaxed part of their
watchfulness, and began to be careless of our
escaping. Labarree and Farnsworth were slight-
ly bound, and my husband had all his liberty.
My sister could sleep without her two Indian
companions, and the whole company appeared
less like prisoners.

In the morning of the eighth day, we were
roused at sunrise. Although the early part of

September is generally blessed with a serene sky and a warm sun, yet we suffered exceedingly by the cold. The mornings were damp and foggy, and the lofty trees and numerous mountains often exclude the sun till noon. Our snakeroot broth, enriched with flour, made a rare breakfast, and gave a little strength to our exhausted limbs. Orders came to ' Munch.' My poor husband took me upon the packsaddle, and we resumed our march. Long before night, despondency had strikingly pictured every countenance. My little son, who had performed the whole journey on foot, was almost lifeless. Mr. Johnson was emaciated, and almost exhausted: often he laid me on the ground, to save his own life and mine ; for my weakness was too great to ride far, without requiring rest. While prostrate upon the earth, and able to speak, I often begged him to leave me there, to end a life which could last but a short time, and would take his with it, if he continued his exertions to save me; but the idea was too shocking. We continued our journey, in a slow, sorrowful mood, till night. Often did I measure a small distance for the sun to run, before I must bid it an eternal adieu. But the same Providence who had brought us so far, and inclined our savage masters to mercy, continued my protector. Farnsworth carried me a small distance, and at last darkness put an end to our painful day's journey. After the customary refreshment, we went to rest. The night was terrible ; the first part was Egyptian darkness, then thunder, and lightening, and rain. On the cold earth, without a cover, our situation may be imagined, but not described. The Indians gave me an additional blanket for my use, and showed some concern for my welfare; but it will ever stand first among modern miracles, that my life was spared.

The morning came, and a bright sun reanimated our drowned spirits. The whole company now resembled a group of ghosts, more than bodily forms. Little did I expect that the light of another day would witness my existence—sensible, that if my own sad diseases did not finish my existence, my husband would be reduced to the woful alternative, of either perishing with me, or leaving me in the woods, to preserve his own life. The horrid yell was given, which was a signal for preparation. Melancholy sat heavily on every countenance, and the tear of woe moistened the sickened cheek of every prisoner. In addition to famine and fatigue, so long a journey, without a shoe for defence, had lacerated and mangled every foot to a shocking degree; travelling was keenly painful. The scanty breakfast was served up; as I was lifting my gill of broth to my cold lips, my master, with a rash hand, pulled it from me, and gave it to my husband, observing, by signs, that he required all the sustenance, to enable him to carry me. I yielded on the supposition that it was a matter of little consequence, whether any thing was bestowed to that body which must soon mingle with its original clay. With sorrow and anguish, we began the ninth day's journey. Before we proceeded far, the Indians signified to us, that we should arrive before night at East Bay, on Lake Champlain. This was a cordial to our drooping spirits, and caused an immediate transition from despair to joy; the idea of arriving at a place of water carriage,

translated us to new life. Those who languished
with sickness, fatigue, or despair, now marched
forward with nervous alacrity. Two Indians were
sent on a hunting scout, who were to meet us at
the bay, with canoes. This seasonable and
agreeable intelligence had every possible effect
that was good; we walked with greater speed,
felt less of the journey, and thought little of our
distress. About the middle of the afternoon the
waters of the lake were seen from a neighboring
eminence; we soon gained the bank, where we
found the two Indians, with four canoes, and a
ground squirrel; a fire was built, and some food
put in preparation. Here my feelings, which had
not been exhilerated so much as the rest of my
fellow-prisoners, were buoyed above despair, and,
for a short time, the pangs of distress lost their
influence. The life, which nine days painful suffering in the wilderness had brought to its last
moment of duration, now started into new existence, and rendered the hour I sat on the shore of
Lake Champlain one of the happiest I ever experienced. Here we were to take passage in
boats, and find relief from the thorny hills and
miry swamps of the damp desart. My husband
could now be relieved from the burden which had
brought him as nigh eternity as myself. My little
children would soon find clothing, and all my
fellow-sufferers would be in a condition to attain
some of life's conveniences. Twelve hours' sailing would waft us to the settlement of civilized
Frenchmen. Considering how much we had endured, few will deem it less than a miracle, that
we were still among the living. My son, of six
years old, had walked barefoot the whole journey.

Farnsworth was shoeless, and carried my eldest daughter. Labarree had to carry and preserve the life of my infant. My sister, owing to her youth and health, had suffered the least. My two little daughters, with only their shifts, and part of one of the three gowns which the savage gave me, were subject to all the damps of morn and night; and Mr. Johnson's situation was pitiably painful; the fatigue of carrying me on the wearying packsaddle had rendered his emaciated body almost a corpse, and his sore feet made him a cripple. The Indians had been surprisingly patient, and often discovered tokens of humanity. At every meal we all shared equal with them, whether a horse or duck composed the bill of fare, and more than once they gave me a blanket, to shelter me from a thunderstorm.

CHAPTER IV.

Crossing the Lake to Crown Point, from thence to St. John's, Chamblee, and to St. Francis Village.

I WILL not detain the reader but a few moments longer in this place, while I eat the leg of a woodchuck, and then request him to take a night's sailing in the canoe with me across the lake, though I sincerely wish him a better passage than I had. No sooner was our repast finished, than the party were divided into four equal parties, for passage. In my boat were two savages, besides my son and infant. I was ordered to lie flat on the bottom of the canoe, and, when pain obliged me to move for relief, I had a rap from a paddle. At daybreak we arrived at a great rock, on the west side of the lake, where we stopped and built a fire. The Indians went to a French house not far distant, and got some meat, bread, and green corn. Although we were not allowed to taste the meat, yet, by the grateful effluvia of the broiling steak, we were finely regaled, and the bread and roast corn were a luxury.

Here the savages, for the first time, gave loud tokens of joy, by hallooing and yelling in a tremendous manner. The prisoners were now introduced to a new school. Little did we expect that the accomplishment of dancing would ever be taught us by the savages. But the war-dance must now be held, and every prisoner that could move must take its awkward steps. The figure consisted of circular motion round the fire; each sang his own music, and the best dancer was the one most violent in motion. The prisoners were taught each a song; mine was, 'Danna witchee natchepung.' My son's was, 'Nar wiscumpton.' The rest I cannot recollect. Whether this task was imposed on us for their diversion, or a religious ceremonial, I cannot say, but it was very painful and offensive. In the forenoon, seven Indians came to us, who were received with great joy by our masters, who took great pleasure in introducing their prisoners. The war-dance was again held; we were obliged to join and sing our songs, while the Indians rent the air with infernal yelling. We then embarked, and arrived at Crown Point about noon. Each prisoner was then led by his master to the residence of the French commander. The Indians kept up their infernal yelling the whole time. We were ordered to his apart-

3 *

ment, and used with that hospitality which charac-
terizes the best part of the nation. We had
brandy in profusion, a good dinner, and a change
of linen. This was luxury indeed, after we had
suffered for the want of these things. None but
ourselves could prize their value. We after dinner were paraded before Mr. Commander, and
underwent examination, after which we were
shown a convenient apartment, where we resided
four days, not subject to the jurisdiction of our
savage masters. Here we received great civilities,
and many presents. I had a nurse, who in a great
measure restored my exhausted strength. My
children wore all decently clothed, and my infant
in particular. The first day, while I was taking a
nap, they dressed it so fantastically, a-la-France,
I refused to own it, when brought to my bedside,
not guessing that I was the mother of such a
strange thing.

On the fourth day, to our great grief and mortification, we were again delivered to the Indians,
who led us to the water side, where we all embarked in one vessel for St. John's. The wind
shifted, after a short sail, and we dropped anchor.
In a little time, a canoe came along side of us, in
which was a white woman, who was bound for
Albany. Mr. Johnson begged her to stop a few
minutes, while he wrote to Col. Lydius, of Albany,
to inform him of our situation, and to request him
to put the same in the Boston newspapers, that
our friends might learn that we were alive. The
woman delivered the letter, and the contents were
published, which conveyed the agreeable tidings
to our friends, that, although prisoners, we were
then alive.

The following letter, in return for the one we sent to Col. Lydius, was the first we received from New England:—

Albany, Nov. 5, 1754.

Sir :—I received yours of the 5th October, with a letter or two for New England, which I forwarded immediately, and have wrote to Boston, in which I urged the government to endeavor to procure your and family's redemption, as soon as conveniency would admit.

I am quite sorry for your doleful misfortune, and hope the just God will endue you with patience to undergo your troubles, and justly use his rewards on the evil doers and authors of your misfortune. Present my service to all the prisoners with you, from him who subscribes himself to be your very humble servant;

JOHN W LYDIUS.

LIEUT. JAMES JOHNSON, Montreal.

After a disagreeable voyage of three days, we made St. John's, the 16th of September, where we again experienced the politeness of a French commander. I, with my child, was kindly lodged in the same room with himself and lady. In the morning we still found misfortune treading close at our heels; we must again be delivered to our savage masters, and take another passage in the boats for Chamblee, when, within three miles of which, Labarree, myself, and child, with our two masters, were put on shore ; we were ignorant of our destiny, and parting from my husband and friends was a severe trial, without knowing whether we were ever to meet them again. We walked on to Chamblee ; here our fears were dissipated, by meeting our friends. In the garrison of this place, we found all the hospitality our necessities required. Here, for the first time after my captivity, I lodged on a bed. Brandy was handed about in large bowls, and we lived in high style. The next morning we were put in the custody of our old masters, who took us to the canoes, in which we had a painful voyage that day, and the following night, to Sorell, where we arrived on the 19th. A hospitable friar came to the shore to see us, and invited us to his house ; he gave us a good breakfast, and drank our better healths in a tumbler of brandy ; he took compassionate notice of my child, and ordered it some suitable food. But the Indians hurried us off before it could eat. He then went with us to the shore, and ordered his servant to carry the food, prepared for the child, to the canoe, where he waited till I fed it. The friar was a genteel man, and gave us his benediction, at parting, in feeling language. We then rowed on till the middle of the afternoon, when we landed on a barren heath, and, by the help of a fire, cooked an Indian dinner ; after which, the war-dance was held, and another infernal yelling. The prisoners were obliged to sing till they were hoarse, and dance round the fire.

We had now arrived within a few miles of the village of St. Francis, to which place our masters belonged. Whenever the warriors return from an excursion against an enemy, their return to the tribe or village must be designated by warlike ceremonial ; the captives or spoil, which may happen to crown their valor, must be conducted in a triumphant form, and decorated to every possible advantage. For this end, we must now submit to painting : their vermillion, with which they were ever supplied, was mixed with bear's-grease, and every cheek, chin, and forehead, must have a dash. We then rowed on within a mile of the town, where we stopped at a French house, to dine ; the prisoners were served with soup meagre and bread. After dinner, two savages proceeded to the village, to carry the glad tidings of our arrival. The whole atmosphere soon resounded from every quarter, with whoops, yells, shrieks, and screams. St. Francis, from the noise that came from it, might be supposed the centre of Pandemonium. Our masters were not backward ; they made every response they possibly could. The whole time we were sailing from the French house, the noise was direful to be heard. Two hours before sunset we came to the landing at the village. No sooner had we landed, than the yelling in the town was redoubled. A cloud of savages, of all sizes and sexes, soon appeared running towards us ; when they reached the boats, they formed themselves into a long parade, leaving a small space, through which we must pass. Each Indian then took prisoner by his hand, and, after ordering him the war-song, began to march through the let. We expected a severe beating, befor through, but were agreeably disappointe we found that each Indian only gave us the shoulder. We were led directly to each taking his prisoner to his ow When I entered my master'r door, I luted me with a large belt of wa master present.d me with anotl put over my shoulders, and cross fore. My new home was not th a large wigwam, without a floor, with a fire in the centre, and only a few water-vessels and dishes, to eat from, made of burch bark, and tools for cookery, made clumsily of wood, for furniture, will not be thought a pleasing residence to one accustomed to civilized life.

CHAPTER V.

Residence at St. Francis. Sale of most of the Pri-soners to the French, and Removal to Montreal.

NIGHT presently came, after our arrival at St. Francis. Those who have felt the gloomy, home-sick feelings, which sadden those hours which a youth passes, when first from a father's house, may judge of part of my sufferings; but, when the rest of my circumstances are added, their conception must fall infinitely short. I now found myself with my infant, in a large wigwam, ac-pahied with two or three warriors, and as squaws, where I must spend the night, and s a year. My fellow-prisoners were dis-ver the town—each one, probably, feel-same gloominess with myself. Hasty-resently was brought forward for sup-nacious bowl of wood, well filled, was central spot, and each one drew near n spoon. As the Indians never use any in their wigwams, my awk-ng my position was a matter of ent to my new companions. The upon their knees, and then sit back upon their heels. This was a posture that I could not imitate. To sit in any other was thought by them indelicate and unpolite. But I advanced to my pudding with the best grace I could—not, however, escaping some of their funny remarks. When the hour for sleep came on, for it would be improper to call it bedtime, where beds were not, I was pointed to a platform, raised half a yard, where, upon a board covered with a blanket, I was to pass the night. The Indians threw themselves down in various parts of the building, in a manner that more resembled cows in a shed, than human beings in a house. In the morning, our breakfast consisted of the relics of the last night; my sister came to see me in the forenoon, and we spent some hours in observations upon our situation, while washing some apparel at a brook. In the afternoon, I, with my infant, was taken to the grand parade, where we found a large collection of the village inhabitants; an aged chief stepped forward into an area, and, after every noise was silenced, and every one fixed in profound attention, he began to harrangue. His manner was solemn; his motions and expression gave me a perfect idea of an orator. Not a breath was heard, and every spectator seemed to reverence what he said. After the speech, my little son was brought to the opposite side of the parade, and a number of blankets laid by his side. It now appeared that his master and mine intended an exchange of prisoners. My master being a hunter, wished for my son, to attend him on his excursions. Each delivered his property with great formality—my son and blankets being an equivalent for myself, child, and wampum. I was

3†

taken to the house of my new master, and found myself allied to the first family; my master, whose name was Gill, was son-in-law to the grand sachem, was accounted rich, had a store of goods, and lived in a style far above the majority of his tribe. He often told me that he had an English heart, but his wife was true Indian blood. Soon after my arrival at his house, the interpreter came to inform me that I was adopted into his family. I was then introduced to the family, and was told to call them brothers and sisters. I made a short reply, expressive of gratitude, for being introduced to a house of high rank, and re-quested their patience while I should learn the customs of the nation. This was scarce over, when the attention of the village was called to the grand parade, to attend a rejoicing, occasioned by the arrival of some warriors, who had brought some scalps. They were carried in triumph on a pole. Savage butchery upon murdered country-men! The sight was horrid. As I retired to my new residence, I could hear the savage yells that accompanied the war-dance. I spent the night in sad reflection.

My time now was solitary beyond description; my new sisters and brothers treated me with the same attention that they did their natural kindred, but it was an unnatural situation to me. I was a novice at making canoes, bunks, and tumplines, which was the only occupation of the squaws; of course, idleness was among my calmities. My fellow-prisoners were as gloomy as myself—igno-rant whether they were to spend their days in this inactive village, or be carried into a war campaign, to slaughter their countrymen, or to be dragged to the cold lakes of the north, in a hunting voyage. We visited each other daily, and spent our time in conjecturing our future destiny.

The space of forty-two years having elapsed, since my residence in St. Francis, it is impossible to give the reader a minute detail of events that occurred while there ; many of them are still forcibly impressed upon my memory, but dates and particulars are now inaccurately treasured up by faint recollection. Mr. Johnson tarried but a few days with me, before he was carried to Montreal, to be sold. My two daughters, sister, and Labarree, were soon after carried to the same place, at different times. Farnsworth was carried by his master on a hunting scout, but, not proving so active in the chase and ambush as they wished, he was returned and sent to Montreal. I now found an increase to my trouble : with only my son and infant, in this strange land, without a prospect of relief, and with all my former trouble lying heavy upon me, disappointment and despair came well nigh being my executioners. In this dilemma, who can imagine my distress, when my little son came running to me one morning, swollen with tears, exclaiming, that the Indians were going to carry him into the woods to hunt ; he had scarcely told the piteous story, before his master came to pull him away ; he threw his little arms around me, begging, in the agony of grief, that I would keep him. The inexorable savage unclenched his hands, and forced him away : the last words I heard, intermingled with his cries, were, 'Ma'am, I shall never see you again.' 'The keenness of my pangs almost obliged me to wish that I never had been a mother. 'Farewell, Sylvanus,' said I; 'God will preserve you.'

It was now the 15th of October. Forty-five days had passed since my captivity, and no prospect but what was darkened with clouds of misfortune. The uneasiness occasioned by indolence was in some measure relieved, by the privilege of making shirts for my brother. At night and morn I was allowed to milk the cows. The rest of the time I strolled gloomily about, looking sometimes into an unsociable wigwam, at others sauntering into the bushes, and walking on the banks of brooks. Once I went to a French house, three miles distant, to visit some friends of my brother's family, where I was entertained politely a week: at another time, I went with a party to fish, accompanied by a number of squaws. My weakness obliged me to rest often, which gave my companions a poor opinion of me; but they showed no other resentment, than calling me 'no good squaw,' which was the only reproach my sister ever gave, when I displeased her. All the French inhabitants I formed an acquaintance with, treated me with that civility which distinguishes the nation; once in particular, being almost distracted with an aching tooth, I was carried to a French physician, across the river, for relief. They prevailed on the Indians to let me visit them a day or two, during which time, their marked attention and generosity claims my warmest gratitude. At parting, they expressed their earnest wishes to have me visit them again.

St. Francis contained about thirty wigwams, which were thrown disorderly into a clump,

There was a church, in which mass was held every night and morning, and every Sunday the hearers were summoned by a bell, and attendance was pretty general. Ceremonies were performed by a French friar, who lived in the midst of them, for the salvation of their souls. He appeared to be in that place, what the legislative branch is in civil governments, and the grand sachem the executive. The inhabitants lived in perfect harmony, and had most of their property in common. They were prone to indolence when at peace, and not remarkable for neatness. They were extremely modest, and apparently averse to airs of courtship. Necessity was the only thing that called them to action; this induced them to plant their corn, and to undergo the fatigues of hunting. Perhaps I am wrong to call necessity the only motive; revenge, which prompts them to war, has great power. I had a numerous retinue of relations, whom I visited daily; but my brother's house being one of the most decent in the village, I fared full as well at home. Among my connexions was a little brother Sabatis, who brought the cows for me, and took particular notice of my child. He was a sprightly little fellow, and often amused me with feats performed with his bow and arrow.

In the early part of November, Mr. Johnson wrote from Montreal, requesting me to prevail on the Indians to carry me to Montreal for sale, as he had made provision for that purpose. I disclosed the matter, which was agreed to by my brother and sister, and on the seventh we set sail in a little bark canoe. While crossing Lake St. Peters, we came nigh landing on the shores of eternity. The waves were raised to an enormous height by the wind, and often broke over the canoe. My brother and sister were pale as ghosts, and we all expected immediate destruction; but the arm of salvation was extended for our relief, and we reached the shore. We were four days in this voyage, and received obliging civilities every night, at French settlements; on the eleventh, we arrived at Montreal, where I had the supreme satisfaction of meeting my husband, children, and friends. Here I had the happiness to find, that all my fellow-prisoners had been purchased by persons of respectability, by whom they were treated with humanity; and all except Polly, of whom I shall say something further, I believe were used very well.

Mr. Du Quesne bought my sister, my eldest daughter was owned by three affluent old maids, by the name of Jaisson, and the other, to wit, Polly, was owned by the mayor of the city. The mayor's lady had her kept out at boarding and nursing. I had information that the child was not well used—that no proper care was taken of her. I set off with a determination to find her, which I did, and on finding her, I found the intelligence which I had received but too true. To see my child in so miserable a plight, gave my mind much trouble. I informed those where she was kept, that I could not think of having her kept in such a manner, and should endeavor to have her taken away, and put where she might have better care taken of her. I went not long after to see her again, but was forbid to see her, by order of the mayor's lady. I thought it very hard that I could not be suffered to see my unhappy child, and was determined, if possible, to get her away. On my returning to my lodging, I immediately went with an interpreter to see the lady. It was with much difficulty that I could even get admittance, so as to speak to her; but, when I did, I collected all my fortitude, and, in the feeling language of a mother, made my suit for liberty to visit my child. But I was denied with a frown! The lady could not see why a poor woman, and a prisoner, as I was, should want to torment herself and child with such fruitless visits! She said that the child was well enough off, and, when it arrived at a suitable age, she should see to it herself! But I expostulated with her, by the interpreter, upbraided her with her cruelty and hardheartedness, and the vanity of her thinking, because I was poor, I had not, or need not have, any love or concern for my child. I requested her to think as a mother, that poverty did not, nor could it ever, erase parental love and affection. I told her that the child was mine, and she had no right to it. We were prisoners, it was true, but I expected we should be exchanged; when I expected that I and my children would return to our native country. I conjured her to think of me on her pillow, and realize the matter, by making my case hers, and consider what torture I must be in, while, in addition to my being a poor prisoner, I was deprived of the privilege of seeing my poor, unhappy child. And much more I said to her, to this effect, to which she seemed to pay some attention, but gave me no favorable answer. I returned to my lodging rather sad and gloomy, though not entirely out of hopes, but what I should finally meet with suc-

4

cess; for I thought that the lady (and a lady indeed she appeared to be) must be lost to all sense of humanity, or else I must have wrought a little upon her feelings, which was my object to do. And in this I was not disappointed; for the next day she sent her servant to the interpreter, for to inform me that I might see my child, and do with it according to my wishes. 'Tell that English woman,' said she, 'I could not sleep last night; her observations broke my heart! She may have her child! I cannot withhold it from her any longer!' And she was as good as her word; for she furnished clothing, and I had my dear little child to myself, and had several presents with it from the lady, and she asked nothing for all her trouble.

I would remark here, that it was fashionable, among the higher class of people in Canada, to have their own children nursed out till they were about three or four years old. They are dressed neat and clean about once a month, and carried to their parents, by the servant, to visit. The other part of the time they are not kept in so clean a manner, by their nurses, as the English people generally are. And perhaps mine was more neglected for being a poor prisoner's child. I also learned that the mayor's lady wished very much to have my child again for her own, as she had had but only one daughter; who had died just before, aged 15 years.

But to return again to my narrative. Mr. Johnson had obtained the privilege of two months' absence on parole, for the purpose of going to New England, to procure cash for the redemption of his family. He sat out on his journey the day after my arrival at Montreal. Mr. Du. Quesne engaged to supply his family with necessaries during his absence, and was to be recompensed at his return. Directly after his departure, I found myself doomed to fresh trouble. The Indians brought me here for the purpose of exchanging me for some Micanaw savages, a tribe with whom they were at war; but, being disappointed in this, they were exorbitant in their demands, and refused to take less than a thousand livres for me and my child. Mr. Du Quesne fixed his offer at seven hundred, which was utterly refused by my savage masters. Their next step was to threaten to carry me back to St. Francis. After half a day's surly deliberation, they concluded to take the offered sum. I was received into Mr. Du Quesne's family. My joy at being delivered from savage captivity was unbounded. From this period, Indians and sufferings were no more to torture me or my family, except the unfortunate Sylvanus. The fond idea of liberty held forth its dazzling pleasures, and the ignorance of future calamities precluded every cloud that could obscure its effulgence. On Mr. Johnson's journey to New England, I rested all my hope, and felt full confidence in being relieved at his return.

In justice to the Indians, I ought to remark, that they never treated me with cruelty to a wanton degree. Few people have survived a situation like mine, and few have fallen into the hands of savages disposed to more lenity and patience. Modesty has ever been a characteristic of every savage tribe—a truth which my whole family will join to corroborate, to the extent of their know-

ledge. As they are aptly called the children of
nature, those who have profited by refinement and
education ought to abate part of the prejudice,
which prompts them to look with an eye of censure
on this untutored race. Can it be said of civilized
conquerors, that they, in the main, are willing to
share with their prisoners the last ration of food,
when famine stares them in the face? Do they
ever adopt an enemy, and salute him by the tender
name of brother? And I am justified in doubting,
whether, if I had fallen into the hands of French
soldiery, so much assiduity would have been shown
to preserve my life.

CHAPTER VI.

*Mr. Johnson's Tour to Boston and Portsmouth, and
the Catastrophe at his return. Arrival at the
Prison in Quebec.*

THE reader will leave me and my family under
the care of our factor a short time, and proceed
with Mr. Johnson. On the 12th of November, he
sat out for Albany, accompanied by two Indians
for pilots, for whose fidelity the commander-in-
chief was responsible. They were to tarry at
Albany till his return. In a short time I had a
letter from Col. Lydius, informing me that he had
safely arrived at Albany, and had gone to Boston.
His first step was to apply to Governer Shirley
for money, to redeem his family and the English
prisoners. Shirley laid his matter before the general assembly, and they granted the sum of ten

pounds, to defray his expenses. He got no further assistance in Massachusetts, and was advised to apply to the government of New Hampshire. Gov. Wentworth laid the matter before the general assembly of that state, and the sum of one hundred and fifty pounds sterling was granted for the purpose of redemption of prisoners. The committee of the general court of New Hampshire gave him the following directions:—

Portsmouth, N. H., Jan. 25, 1755.

Mr. James Johnson:—Sir, agreeable to your letter to the secretary, of the 16th instant, you have enclosed a letter to Col. Cornelius Cuyler, Esq., in which you will observe we have given you credit for letters on his acquaintance in Canada, to furnish you with credit to the amount of 150 pounds sterling. We therefore advise you to proceed to Albany, and, on your arrival there, deliver the said letter to Col. Cuyler, and take from him such credit as he shall give you, on some able person or persons in Canada; and, when you are thus furnished, you will then proceed to Canada, and there negociate, in the best and most frugal manner you can, the purchasing such, and so many captives, as you may hear of, that have been taken from any part of this province, taking care that the aforesaid sum, agreeable to the grant of the general assembly here, be distributed to and for the purchasing all the said captives that are to be come at, in the most equal and exact manner, that none may be left there for want of their quota of said money. The captives' names, and places from whence taken, that we have information of, you have herewith a list of, for your direction. You 'are to keep an exact account of the distribution of this money, in order to your future discharge.

If Col. Cuyler should not be living, or refuse you his good offices in this affair, you are then to apply to the Hon. —————— Saunders, Esq., mayor of the city of Albany, or any other person that can give you credit at Canada, and leave with them our letter to Col. Cuyler, which shall oblige us to pay the said sum or sums, mentioned in the said letter, to such person, and in the same way and manner as we have obliged ourselves to pay him.

We are your friends,

THEODORE ATKINSON,
S. WIBIRT,
MESHECH WEARE,
BENJ. SHERBURNE, Jun.
} Com.

A List of the Captives taken from the Province of New Hampshire, by the St. Francis Indians, in the Summer of 1754.

From Charlestown, on Connecticut River, James Johnson, his wife, and four children. Peter Labarree. Ebenezer Farnsworth. Miriam Willard.

From Merrimac River, Nathaniel Mallon, his wife, and three children. Robert Barber. Samuel Scribner. Enos Bishop.

In addition to this letter of credit, Governor Wentworth gave him the following passport :—

Province of New Hampshire, in New England.

By His Excellency, Benning Wentworth, Esq.,
  Captain General, Governor, and Com-
  mander in Chief, in and over his Brit-
L. S. tanic Majesty's Province of New Hamp-
    shire aforesaid, and Vice Admiral of the
    same, and Surveyor General of all his
    Majesty's Woods in North America :—

Whereas the St. Francis and other Indians
did, in the summer last past, captivate sundry of
his majesty's subjects, inhabitants of this province,
and have, as I have been informed, sold the same
to the subjects of the French king in Canada,
where they are now detained in servitude, and
having had application made to me, by Mr. James
Johnson, of Charlestown, within this province, one
of the said captives, who obtained leave to come
to this country, in order to purchase his own and
other captives' liberty—for letters of safe passport, I do hereby require and command all officers, civil and military, as well as all other persons, that they offer no lett or hindrance to the
said James Johnson or his company, but contra-
wise, that they afford him all necessary despatch
in said journey through this province.

And I do hereby also desire, that all his majesty's subjects, of his several other governments,
through which the said Johnson may have occasion to travel, may treat him with that civility that
becometh.

I also hereby earnestly entreat the governor
general, and all other officers, ministers, and subjects of his most Christian majesty, governing and
4 *

inhabiting the country and territories of Canada aforesaid, that they would respectively be aiding and assisting to the said James Johnson, in the aforesaid negociation—hereby engaging to return the same civility and kindness to any of his most Christian majesty's officers and subjects, when thereto requested, by any of his governors or proper officers. In token of which, I have caused the public seal of. the province, of New Hampshire aforesaid, to be hereunto affixed, this 25th day of January, in the 28th year of the reign of our sovereign lord, George the Second, of Great Britain, France, and Ireland, King, Defender of the Faith, &c.   BENNING WENTWORTH.
By his Excellency's Command,
          THEODORE ATKINSON, Sec'y.
     Anno Domini, 1755.

With these credentials, Mr. Johnson proceeded with alacrity to Boston, procured Gov. Shirley's passport, and set forward to Worcester, on his return back. While there, he was greatly astonished at receiving the following letter from Governor Shirley :—

          Boston, February 15, 1755.
MR. JOHNSON :—there have some things happened in our public affairs, since your going from Boston with my letters to the governor of Canada, and intelligence come of the motions of the French in Canada, for further invading his majesty's territories on the frontiers of New York and New Hampshire, as make it unsafe for you, as well as for the public, to proceed at present on your journey to Quebec; and therefore I expect that

you do forthwith, upon receiving this letter, return
back, and lay aside all thoughts of going forward
on this journey, till you have my leave, or the
leave of Governor Wentworth, to whom I shall
write, and inform him of what I have undertook
to do in this matter, in which his majesty's service
is so much concerned.   W. SHIRLEY.
  MR. JAMES JOHNSON.

On the receipt of this letter, he returned with a
heavy heart to Boston, and was positively ordered
by Shirley to stay till further orders. His situation now was really deplorable. His parole,
which was only for two months, must be violated,
his credit in Canada lost, his family exposed to
the malice of exasperated Frenchmen, and all his
good prospects at an end. After using every exertion in Boston, for leave to recommence his
journey, and spending the rest of the winter, and
all the spring, he found his efforts were in vain.
During this time, my situation grew daily distressing. Mr. Du Quesne made honorable provision
for myself, sister, and child, till the expiration of
my husband's parole; the two Indians were then
sent to Albany, to pilot him back; after waiting
some time, and learning nothing about him, they
returned. Previous to this, I had been treated
with great attention and civility, dined frequently
in the first families, received cards to attend them
on parties of pleasure, and was introduced to a
large and respectable acquaintance. As an unfortunate woman, I received those general tokens
of generosity which flow from a humane people.
Among the presents which I received, was one of
no small magnitude, from Captains Stowbrow

and Vambram, two gentlemen who were delivered
by Major Washington, as hostages, when he, with
the Virginia troops, surrendered to the French
and Indians. In compliance with their billet, I
waited on them one morning, and at parting received a present of 148 livres. Mr. St. Agne, a
French gentleman of fortune and distinction, be-
side frequent proofs of his goodness, gave me at
one time 48 livres. In his family I formed an intimate acquaintance with a young English lady,
who was captured by the Indians in the province
of Maine, and sold to him. She was used with
parental tenderness, and shared the privileges of
his children; she, with his daughter, frequently
came in their morning carriage, to ride with my
sister and me. Gratitude to my numerous benefactors pleads loudly in favor of inserting all their
names, and particularizing every act of generosity. If I omit it, it must not be imagined that I
have forgotten their charity; it has left an impres-
sion on my heart, that can only be erased with my
existence.

While in Mr. Du Quesne's family, my ltttle
daughter was very unwell, and the superstitious
people were convinced that she would either die,
or be carried off by the devil, unless baptized. I
yielded to their wishes, and they prepared for the
ceremony with all the appendages annexed to
their religion. Mr. Du Quesne was godfather,
and the young English lady godmother; by Mrs.
Du Quesne's particular request, she was christen-
ed Louise, after herself, to which I added the
name of Captive.

The return of the Indians without Mr. Johnson
boded no good to me. I observed, with pain, the

gradual change in my friends, from coldness to neglect, and from neglect to contempt. Mr. Du Quesne, who had the most delicate sense of honor, supposed that he had designedly broken his parole, and abused his confidence; he refused to grant me further assistance, or even to see my face. I now found myself friendless and alone; not a word had I heard from Mr. Johnson—not a word had I heard from my little son with the Indians. Affliction lowered upon me with all its horrors; in this dilemma, my sister and I agreed to take a small room, and support ourselves till our little store of cash was expended, and then have recourse to our needles.

In the beginning of April, the Indians made a second tour to Albany, in quest of Mr. Johnson; and again returned without him. I wrote to Col. Lydius for information, but he could tell nothing. Darkness increased; but I summoned all my resolution, and indulged the fond hope of being soon relieved. We kept our little room till June, when I had the happiness to hear that my husband was without the city, waiting for permission to come in. He was conducted in by a file of men : his presence banished care and trouble, and turned the tear of sorrow to the effusion of joy. After the joy of meeting had subsided, he related his sad fate in New England. He finally got permission from Gov. Wentworth to come privately, by the way of Albany, where he took his bills, drawn by Mr. Cuyler, on Mr. St. Luc Lucorne, and Mr. Rine Du Quesne. The face of affairs in Canada had materially changed; during his absence, a new governor had been sent over, and various manœuvres in politics had taken place,

which were very injurious to him. Had the old
governor tarried, his absence would have probably
been excused. But Mons. Vandrieul was ignorant of the conditions on which he went home,
and could not admit apologies for the breach of
his parole. Our disappointment and mortification
were severe, when we found our bills protested.
This reduced us at once to a beggarly state. The
evil was partially remedied by St. Luc Lucorne's
lending us paper money, while we could send
some Indians to Mr. Cuyler for silver. Mr. Johnson received orders to settle his affairs with all
possible despatch.

Spirited preparations were now making for war.
General Dieskau arrived from France with an army, and Montreal was a scene of busy confusion.
We were completing our settlements with our paper, expecting to have full permission to go home,
when the Indians returned. But the measure of
our misery was not yet full. In the beginning of
July, Mr. Johnson was put into jail. Terrible to
me was this unexpected stroke ; without money,
credit, or friends, I must now roam the streets,
without a prospect of relief from the cloud of misfortune that hung over me. In a few days, the
faithful Indians, who had been sent to Mr. Cuyler
for the silver, returned with 438 dollars, with an
order on St. Luc Lucorne for 700 additional livres;
but he took the whole into possession, and we
never after received a penny from him.

Half distracted, and almost exhausted with despair and grief, I went to the governor, to paint
our distress and ask relief. I found him of easy
access, and he heard my lamentable story with
seeming emotion ; his only promise was to take

.care of us, and at parting he gave me.a crown, to
buy milk' for.my babes. ' Ignorant of our destiny,
my sister and I kept our little room, and were fortunate enough to get subsistence from day to day
—often going to the gloomy prison, to see my poor
husband, whose misfortunes in Boston had brought
him to this wretchedness.

.Our own misfortunes had taught us how to feel
for the sufferings of others, and large demands
were now made on our sympathetic powers. Just
as we were plunged into this new distress, a scout
of savages brought a number of prisoners into
Montreal, which were our old friends and acquaintance.* Our meeting was a scene of sorrow and
melancholy pleasure.

All were now flocking to the standard of war.
The Indians came from all quarters, thirsting for
English blood, and receiving instruction from the
French. A number of tribes, with all their horrid
weapons of war, paraded one morning before the
general's house, and held the war-dance, and filled
the air with infernal yells ; after which, in a for-
mal manner, they took the hatchet against the

---

* Two children from Mr. H. Grout's family, and two children
belonging to Mrs. Howe, the fair captive, celebrated in Col.
Humphrey's life of Putnam. Their names were Polly and Submit Phips. Mrs. Howe was then a prisoner at St. John's, with
six other children, and one Garfield. They were all taken at
Hinsdale. Mrs. Howe's daughters were purchased by Mons.
Vandrieul, the governor, and had every attention paid their education. After a year's residence in Montreal, they were sent to
the grand nunnery in Quebec, where my sister and I made them
a visit ; they were beautiful girls, cheerful, and well taught.
We here found two aged English ladies, who had been taken in
former wars. One, by the name of Wheelwright, who had a
brother in Boston, on whom she requested me to call, if ever I
went to that place ; I complied with her request afterwards, and
received many civilities from her brother.

4 †

English, and marched for the field of battle. Alas! my poor countrymen, thought I, how many of you are to derive misery from these monsters. On the 22d of July, Mr. Johnson was taken from the jail, and, with myself and our two youngest children, were ordered on board a vessel for Quebec. To leave our friends at Montreal was a distressing affair ; my sister's ransom had been paid, but she could not go with us. She went into the family of the lieutenant governor, where she supported herself with her needle. My eldest daughter was still with the three old maids, who treated her tenderly. Labarree and Farnsworth had paid the full price of their redemption, but were not allowed to go home. Not a word had we heard yet from poor Sylvanus. We parted in tears, ignorant of our destination, but little thinking that we were to embark for a place of wretchedness and woe. After two days' good sailing, we arrived at Quebec, and were all conducted directly to jail.

CHAPTER VII.

Six Months' residence in the Criminal Jail, and removal to the Civil Prison.

WE now, to our indescribable pain, found the fallacy of Mr. Governor's promises for our welfare. This jail was a place too shocking for description. In one corner sat a poor being, half dead with the smallpox ; in another were some lousy blankets and straw ; in the centre stood a few dirty dishes, and the whole presented a scene miserable to view. The terrors of starvation, and the fear of suffocating in filth, were overpowered by the more alarming evil of the smallpox, which none of us had had. But there was no retreat; resignation was our only resource. The first fortnight we waited anxiously for the attack of the disease, in which time we were supported by a small piece of meat a day, which was stewed with some rusty crusts of bread, and brought to us in a pail that swine would run from. The straw and lousy blankets were our only lodging, and the rest of our furniture consisted of some wooden blocks for seats. On the fifteenth day I was taken with the smallpox, and removed to the hospital, leaving my husband and two children in the horrid prison. In two days, Mr. Johnson put my youngest child, Captive, out to nurse. The woman kept the child but a few days, before she returned it, owing to a mistrust, that she should not get her pay.

My husband brought the child to me at the hospital, and told me the sad tale; and, after bathing the poor little infant in tears, I thought and said, 'The task is too hard! had it been the will of God to have taken the child away, it might have alleviated some part of our trouble.' But my husband immediately checked my murmurings, and said, 'Be still, and let us not complain of the providence of God; for we know not for what purpose this dear child is so miraculously preserved. It may yet be the greatest comfort to us in our old age, should we arrive to it.' And much more he said to this effect, which I do not so particularly recollect. And I am constrained to say, that I have had the happiness of finding his predictions fully exemplified.—But to return to my narrative. Should the dear little thing remain in prison, certain death must inevitably be her portion. My husband was therefore reduced to the sad necessity of requesting the woman to carry it to the lord intendant, and tell him that he must either allow her a compensation for keeping it, or it must be left at his door. The good woman dressed it decently, and obeyed her orders. Mr. Intendant smiled at her story, and took the child in his arms, saying it was a pretty little English devil—it was a pity it should die. He ordered his clerk to draw an order for its allowance, and she took good care of it till the last of October, except a few days, while it had the smallpox.

A few days after I left the prison, Mr. Johnson and my other daughter were taken with symptoms, and came to the hospital to me. It is a singular instance of divine interposition, that we all recovered from this malignant disease. We were remanded to prison, but were not compelled to our former rigid confinement. Mr. Johnson was allowed, at certain times, to go about the city, in quest of provision. But, on the 20th of October, St. Luc Lucorne arrived from Montreal, with the news of Dieskau's defeat; he had, ever since my husband's misfortune about his parole, been his persecuting enemy. By his instigation we were all put directly to close prison.

The ravages of the smallpox reduced us to the last extremity, and the fœtid prison, without fire or food, added bitterness to our distress. Mr. Johnson preferred a petition to the lord intendant, stating our melancholy situation. I had the liberty of presenting it myself, and, by the assistance of Mr. Perthieur, the interpreter, in whom we

ever found a compassionate friend, we got some
small relief." About the first of November, I was
taken violently ill of a fever, and was carried to
the hospital, with my daughter Captive. After a
month's residence there, with tolerable good attendance, I recovered from my illness, and went
back to my husband. While at the hospital, I
found an opportunity to convey the unwelcome
tidings of our deplorable situation to my sister at
Montreal, charging her to give my best love to my
daughter Susanna, and to inform our fellow-prisoners, Labarree and Farnsworth, that our good
wishes awaited them. Not a word had we yet
heard from poor Sylvanus.

Winter now began to approach, and the severe
frosts of Canada operated keenly upon our feelings. Our prison was a horrid defence from the
blasts of December; with two chairs and a heap
of straw, and two lousy blankets, we may well be
supposed to live uncomfortable; but, in addition
to this, we had but one poor fire a day, and the
iron grates gave free access to the chills of the
inclement sky. A quart bason was the only thing
allowed us to cook our small piece of meat and
dirty crusts in, and it must serve at the same time
for table furniture. In this sad plight—a prisoner
—in jail—winter approaching—conceive, reader,
for I cannot speak, our distress.

Our former benevolent friends, Capt. Stowbrow
and Vambram, had the peculiar misfortune to be
cast into a prison opposite to us. Suspicion of
having corresponded with their countrymen, was
the crime with which they were charged. Their
misfortune did not preclude the exertion of generosity; they frequently sent us, by the waiting-

maid, bottles of wine, and articles of provision.
But the malice of Frenchmen had now arrived to
such a pitch against all our country, that we must
be deprived of these comforts. These good men
were forbidden their offices of kindness, and our
intercourse was entirely prohibited. We however
found means, by a stratagem, to effect, in some
measure, what could not be done by open dealing.
When the servants were carrying in our daily
supplies, we slipped into the entry, and deposited
our letters in an ash-box, which were taken by
our friends, they leaving one at the same time for
us; this served, in some measure, to amuse a dull
hour. Sometimes we diverted ourselves by the
use of Spanish cards; as Mr. Johnson was ignorant of the game, I derived no inconsiderable
pleasure from instructing him. But the vigilance
of our keepers increased, and our paper and ink
were withheld. We had now been prisoners
seventeen months, and our prospects were changing from bad to worse; five months had elapsed
since our confinement in this horrid receptacle,
except the time we lingered in the hospital. Our
jailer was a true descendant from Pharoah; but,
urged by impatience and despair, I softened him
so much as to get him to ask Mr. Perthieur to call
on us. When the good man came, we described
our situation in all the moving terms which our
feelings inspired, which, in addition to what he
saw, convinced him of the reality of our distress.
He proposed asking an influential friend of his to
call on us, who, perhaps, would devise some mode
for our relief. The next day the gentleman came
to see us; he was one of those good souls who
ever feel for others' woes. He was highly affronted

with his countrymen for reducing us to such distress, and declared that the lord intendant himself should call on us, and see the extremities to which he had reduced us; he sent from his own house, that night, a kettle, some candles, and each of us a change of linen.

The next day, January 8th, 1756, Mr. Intendant came to see us; he exculpated himself by saying that we were put there by the special order of Mons. Vaudrieul, the governor-in-chief, and that he had no authority to release us. But he would convey a letter from Mr. Johnson to monsieur, which might have the desired effect. The letter was accordingly written, stating our troubles, and beseeching relief—likewise praying that our son might be got from the Indians and sent to us, with our daughter and sister from Montreal. The governor returned the following obliging letter:—

TRANSLATION.

I HAVE received, sir, your letter, and am much concerned for the situation you are in. I write to Mr. Longieul, to put you and your wife in the civil jail. Mr. L. Intendant will be so good as to take some notice of the things you stand in need of, and to help you. As to your boy, who is in the hands of the Indians, I will do all that is in my power to get him, but I do not hope to have a good success in it. Your child in town, and your sister-in-law, are well. If it is some opportunity of doing you some pleasure, I will make use of it; unless some reason might happen that hinder and stop the effects of my good will. If you had not before given some cause of being suspected, you

5

should be at liberty. I am, sir, your most humble
servant, VAUDRIEUL.

From the receipt of this letter, we dated our
escape from direful bondage. Mr. Intendant ordered us directly to the new jail, called the civil
prison, where our accommodations were infinitely
better. We had a decent bed, candles, fuel, and
all the conveniences belonging to prisoners of
war. Mr. Johnson was allowed fifteen pence per
day, on account of a lieutenant's commission
which he held under George the Second, and I
was permitted to go once a week into the city, to
purchase necessaries, and a washerwoman was
provided for my use. We were not confined to
the narrow limits of a single room, but were restrained only by the bounds of the jail-yard. Our
situation formed such a contrast with what we
endured in the gloomy criminal jail, that we imagined ourselves the favorites of fortune, and in
high life.

CHAPTER VIII.

*Residence in the Civil Jail, and occurrences till the
twentieth of July*, 1757.

To be indolent from necessity, has ever been
deemed a formidable evil. No better witnesses
than ourselves can testify the truth of the remark,
although our lodgings were now such as we envied a month before ; yet, to be compelled to continual idleness, was grievous to be borne. We
derived some amusement from the cultivation of

a small garden, within the jail-yard ; but a continued sameness of friends and action, rendered our
time extremely wearisome.

About a month after our arrival at this new
abode, one Capt. Milton, with his crew, who, with
their vessel, were taken at sea, were brought prisoners of war to the same place. Milton was
lodged in our apartment ; he had all the rude,
boisterous airs of a seaman, without the least trait
of a gentleman, which rendered him a very troublesome companion. His impudence was consummate, but that was not the greatest evil ; while
some new recruits were parading before the prison, one day, Milton addressed them in very improper language from our window, which was
noticed directly by city authority, who, supposing
it to be Mr. Johnson, ordered him into the dun-
geon. Deeply affected by this new trouble, I
again called on my friend, Mr. Perthieur, who,
after having ascertained the facts, got him released. Mr. Milton was then put into other quarters.

A new jailer, who had an agreeable lady for
his wife, now made our situation still more happy.
My little daughters played with hers, and learned
the French language. But my children were
some trouble ; the eldest, Polly, could slip out into
the street under the gate, and often came nigh
being lost. I applied to the centinel, and he kept
her within proper bounds.

Capt. M'Neil and his brother, from Boston,
were brought to us as prisoners ; they informed
us of the state of politics in our own country, and
told us some interesting news about some of our
friends at home.

In the morning of the 13th of August, our jailer,

with moon-eyes, came to congratulate us on the taking of Oswego by the French. We entered little into his spirit of joy, preferring much to hear good news from the other side. We were soon visited by some of the prisoners who had surrendered. Col. Schuyler was in the number, who, with the gentlemen in his suit, made us a generous present.

The remainder of the summer and fall of 1756 passed off without any sensible variation. We frequently heard from Montreal; my sister was very well situated, in the family of the lieutenant governor, and my eldest daughter was caressed by her three mothers. Could I have heard from my son, half my trouble would have ended.

In December I was delivered of a son, which lived but a few hours, and was buried under the Cathedral Church.

In the winter I received a letter from my sister, containing the sad tidings of my father's death. He was killed the 16th of June, 1756, about fifty rods east from the main street in Charlestown, on the same lot on which my youngest brother now lives. My father and my brother, Moses Willard, were repairing some fence on the rear of the lots, and the Indians, being secreted in the bushes a small distance from them, fired upon them, and shot my father dead on the spot. They then sprang to catch my brother; he ran for the fort, and there being a rise of ground to pass towards the fort, the Indian that followed him, finding that he could not catch him, sent his spear, which pierced his thigh, with which he ran to the fort. He is now living in Charlestown, and still carries the scar occasioned by the wound.

The melancholy tidings of the death of my father, in addition to my other afflictions, wore upon me sensibly, and too much grief reduced me to a weak condition. I was taken sick, and carried to the hospital, where, after a month's lingering illness, I found myself able to return.

The commencement of the year 1757 passed off without a prospect of liberty. Part of our fellow-prisoners were sent to France, but we made no voyage out of the jail-yard. About the first of May, we petitioned Mons. Vaudrieul, to permit our sister to come to us. Our prayer was granted; and in May we had the pleasure of seeing her, after an absence of two years. She had supported herself by her needle, in the family of the 'lieutenant governor, where she was treated extremely well; and received a present of four crowns, at parting.

Impatient of confinement, we now made another attempt to gain our liberty. Mr. Perthieur conducted us to the house of the lord intendant, to whom we petitioned in pressing terms, stating, that we had now been prisoners almost three years, and had suffered every thing but death, and that would be our speedy portion, unless we had relief. His lordship listened with seeming pity, and promised to lay our case before the head man at Montreal, and give us an answer in seven days; at the expiration of which time, we had a permit to leave the prison. It is not easy to describe the effect of such news; those only, who have felt the horrors of confinement, can figure to themselves the happiness we enjoyed, when breathing once more the air of liberty. We took lodgings in town, where we tarried till the first of June, when a cartel ship arrived, to carry prisoners to England for an exchange. Mr. Johnson wrote an urgent letter to Mons. Vaudrieul, praying that his family might be included with those who were to take passage. Monsieur wrote a very encouraging letter back, promising that he and his family should sail, and that his daughter, Susanna, should be sent to him. He concluded by congratulating him on his good prospects, and ordering the governor of Quebec to afford us his assistance. This letter was dated June the 27th.

That the reader may the better realize our situation and feelings on this occasion, the copies of the letters are here inserted :—

Sir :—A report being current in town, that all the English prisoners were exchanged, and are to be sent off soon, made me apply to Mr. Perthieur, to know of him whether I was included. He told me that he knew nothing of the affair ; this makes me take the liberty to apply to your excellency, to pray you to have compassion on my distressed situation, and to send me away with others. It is now almost three years that I have been a prisoner with my family, which has already reduced me to extreme want ; and, unless your excellency pities me, I am likely to continue miserable forever. Were I all alone, the affair would not be so melancholy ; but having a wife, and sister, and four children, involved in my misfortune, makes it the more deplorable. And, to add to all my misery, my boy is still in the hands of the savages, notwithstanding I rely upon the letter your excellency did me the honor to condescend to write me, to assure me of your endeavors in withdrawing him out of their hands. And I must therefore once more take the liberty to entreat you to do it, and send him down here, as well as my girl, still at Montreal, and their ransom shall be immediately paid.

As I have your excellency's parole, to be one of the first prisoners sent away, I will not give myself leave to doubt or fear that I shall not—and your excellency well knows, that your predecessor, Mr. D'Longueille, gave me his, that, upon returning from New England, with the ransom of myself and family, I should be at liberty; nevertheless, I was not, owing to want of opportunity.

Your excellency made me the same promise, and the occasion now presenting itself, I well know that I have only to put you in mind of it, in order to the gaining of my desire.

Should it be impossible to get my children with me, (though that would be the greatest of misfortunes,) yet that should not hinder me from going myself, in expectation of *peace*, when I might once more return and fetch them myself.

I hope your excellency will easily forgive the trouble my miserable situation obliges me to give you, and that you will, with your wonted goodness, grant my request.

I am, with profound esteem,
Sir, your most humble, and
most obedient servant,

Mons. D'Vaudrieul. James Johnson.

Quebec, 21st June, 1757.

ANSWER TO THE FOREGOING.—TRANSLATION.

Montreal, June 27, 1757.

Sir :—I have received your letter of the current

5 †

month. I will consent, with pleasure, to your being sent back to England in the packet-boat which I am about to dispatch with some English prisoners. For this purpose, I will send your daughter to Quebec by the first vessel. I am glad to learn that you are in a situation to pay her ransom. I wish that you might find the same facility, on the part of the savages, to get your son out of their hands. When I shall have despatched your daughter, I will write to Mons. D'Longueil to send you back, with your family, after you shall have satisfied the persons who have made advances for their recovery from the savages. I am, sir, your affectionate servant, VAUDRIEUL.

MR. JAMES JOHNSON.

This tide of good fortune almost wiped away the remembrance of three years' adversity. We began our preparations for embarkation with alacrity. Mr. Johnson wrote St. Luc Lucorne for the seven hundred livres due on Mr. Cuyler's order, but his request was, and still is, unsatisfied. This was a period big with every thing propitious and happy. The idea of leaving a country where I had suffered the keenest distress during two months and a half with the savages, been bowed down by every mortification and insult which could arise from the misfortunes of my husband in New England, and where I had spent two years in sickness and despair, in a prison too shocking to mention, contributed to fill the moment with all the happiness which the benevolent reader will conceive my due, after sufferings so intense; to consummate the whole, my daughter was to be returned to my arms, who had been absent more than two years. There was a good prospect of our son's being released from the Indians. The whole formed such a lucky combination of fortunate events, that the danger of twice crossing the ocean, to gain our native shore, vanished in a moment. My family were all in the same joyful mood, and hailed the happy day when we should sail for England.

But little did we think that this sunshine of prosperity was so soon to be darkened by the heaviest clouds of misfortune.

I am not in the habit of placing much dependence on dreams, but the one I shall now relate has been so completely followed, in the course of my great misfortune, I have thought proper to insert it, for the further amusement, if not the satisfaction, of the reader. I thought our friend, Mr. Perthieur, came with a paper in his hand, and delivered it to me. On opening the paper, I found two rings, the one a very beautiful gold dress ring, the other a mourning ring, which were presents, sent, as he said, to me. In putting the dress ring on my finger, I broke it into many pieces, and it fell down, and I could not find the pieces again. The mourning ring I kept whole, and put it on my finger. But when I awoke, behold, it was a dream! I informed my husband of it in the morning, and said to him, I much fear some further misfortune will happen to us. While I was in the civil jail, this dream occurred, and whether it was a prelude to what follows, the reader will judge for himself.

Three days before the appointed hour for sailing, the ship came down from Montreal, without my daughter; in a few moments I met Mr. Perthieur, who told me that counter orders had come, and Mr. Johnson must be retained a prisoner; only my two little daughters, sister, and myself, could go. This was calamity indeed; to attempt such a long, wearisome voyage, without money and without acquaintance, and to leave a husband and two children in the hands of enemies, was too abhorrent for reflection. But it was an affair of importance, and required weighty consideration. Accordingly, the next day a solemn council of all the prisoners in the city was held at the coffee-house. Col. Schuyler was president, and, after numerous arguments for and against were heard, it was voted, by a large majority, that I should go. I, with hesitation, gave my consent. Some, perhaps, will censure the measure as rash, and others may applaud my courage; but I had so long been accustomed to danger and distress, in the most menacing forms they could assume, that I was now almost insensible to their threats; and this act was not a little biased by desperation. Life could no longer retain its value, if lingered out in the inimical regions of Canada. In Europe, I should at least find friends, if not acquaintance; and, among the numerous vessels bound to America, I might chance to get a passage. But then, to leave a tender husband, who had so long, at the hazard of his life, preserved my own—to part, perhaps forever, from two children, put all my resolution to the test, and shook my boasted firmness.

Col. Schuyler, whom we ever found our benevolent friend, promised to use his influence for Mr. Johnson's release, and for the redemption of our children.

On the 20th of July, we went on board the vessel, accompanied by Mr. Johnson, who went with us to take leave. We were introduced to the captain, who was a gentleman, and a person of great civility; he showed us the best cabin, which was to be the place of our residence, and, after promising my husband that the voyage should be made as agreeable to me as possible, he gave orders for weighing anchor. The time was now come that we must part. Mr. Johnson took me by the hand —our tears imposed silence—I saw him step into the barge—but my two little children, sister, and myself, were bound for Europe.

We fell down the river St. Lawrence but a small distance that night. The next morning, the captain, with a cheerful countenance, came to our cabin, and invited us to rise and take our leave of Quebec; none but myself complied, and I gazed, as long as sight would permit, at the place where I had left my dearest friend.

CHAPTER IX.

Voyage to Plymouth.—Occurrences.—Sailing from Plymouth to Portsmouth; from thence, by the way of Cork, to New York.

ALL my fears and affliction did not prevent my feeling some little joy at being released from the jurisdiction of Frenchmen. I could pardon the Indians for their vindictive spirit, because they had no claim to the benefits of civilization. But the French, who give lessons of politeness to the rest of the world, can derive no advantage from the plea of ignorance. The blind superstition, which is inculcated by their monks and friars, doubtless stifles, in some measure, the exertion of pity towards their enemies; and the common herd, which includes almost seven eighths of their number, have no advantages from education. To these sources, I attribute most of my sufferings. But I found some benevolent friends, whose generosity I shall ever recollect with the warmest gratitude.

The commencement of the voyage had every favorable presage; the weather was fine, the sailors cheerful, and the ship in good trim. My accommodations in the captain's family were very commodious; a boy was allowed me, for my particular use. We sailed with excellent fortune till the 19th of August, when we hove in sight of old Plymouth, and at 4 o'clock in the afternoon dropped anchor.

The next day all but myself and family were taken from the vessel; we felt great anxiety at being left, and began to fear that fortune was not willing to smile on us, even on these shores. We waited in despair thirty or forty hours, and found no relief. The captain, observing our despondency, began his airs of gaiety, to cheer us; he assured us that we should not suffer—that if the English would not receive us, he would take us to France, and make us happy. But at last an officer came on board, to see if the vessel was prepared for the reception of French prisoners. We related to him our situation; he conducted us on shore, and applied to the admiral for directions, who ordered us lodgings, and the king's allowance of two shillings sterling per day, for our support. Fortunately we were lodged in a house where resided Captain John Tufton Mason, whose name will be familiar to the inhabitants of New Hampshire, on account of his patent. He very kindly interested himself in our favor, and wrote to Messrs. Thomlinson and Apthorp, agents at London for the province of New Hampshire, soliciting their assistance in my behalf. We tarried at Plymouth but a fortnight, during which time I received much attention, and had to gratify many inquisitive friends with the history of my sufferings. There was one little circumstance that took place while we were at Plymouth, which perhaps will be pleasing to some of my young readers. My little daughter, Captive, had completely acquired the French tongue, so as to be very pert and talkative in it, but she could not speak a word of English. She had been accustomed, at Quebec, to go to market, or any where among the shops, just as she pleased, to buy biscuit, gingerbread, or any such thing that she wanted; and although she used to carry her money, to pay for whatever she bought, yet she generally brought it back again, and sometimes more with it. Of course, she grew very bold; for as she knew nothing of danger, so she feared nothing; and although the sentinels would sometimes use very rough language to her, and threaten to run her through with the bayonet, yet she could return the same language to them, and as they never had hurt her, so she did not believe they ever would; and, being lawless, she went where she had a mind to. Polly, remembering the English tongue, never obtained the French so as to speak it flu-

ently. After we had taken lodgings at Plymouth,
Captive appeared to be very much put out because
she could not make the English understand her;
nor could she any better understand them; and
she imputed it altogether to their ignorance and
impertinence. The lady of the house gave Polly
a biscuit, which being observed by Captive, she
wanted one also. Polly offered her part of hers,
but she would not touch it; she wanted a whole
one, but could not make her want known. The
lady offered her other things, which only vexed
her. Being very much fatigued and unwell, I had
laid down in my chamber, in order to get some
rest, when my little Captive came up to me with
this bitter complaint, and said the lady was the
most *impertinent* woman she ever saw. She had
given Polly a biscuit, and had not given her any,
and when she asked her for one she would offer
her something else. Why, my dear, said I, you
are a little French girl, and these are English people; the lady did not understand you; they do
not talk here as they do in Quebec. But Captive
was very much vexed, and had much to say,
which I think not proper to recite, and finally
concluded by saying she would go to market 'and
buy some biscuit for herself. Why, my child,
continued, I, you cannot find the market here;
you will get lost, or the market women will take
you and carry you off and sell you, and I shall
never see you again. And with this conversation
I pacified her, as I supposed, and fell asleep.
When I awoke, not observing her immediately, I
enquired, ' Where is my Captive ?' ' I do not
know,' said Polly; ' she came down stairs a little
while ago, and said she would go to market, but I

told her she must not, and I have not seen her since.' 'The Lord have mercy,' said I, 'she is gone, and she will be lost, if she is not sought after immediately.' On enquiry of a market woman, she said she had seen a little girl, in a very singular dress, such an one as she had never seen before, almost half a mile off; she spoke to her, but she gave her no answer. I immediately sent a servant after her. She was completely dressed in the French fashion, which attracted the notice of every one that saw her. The servant found her returning home. She had got her *maushum,* which is a little sack or bag, hanging from the left shoulder, full of biscuit, and appeared to be very happy until the servant met her. But her joy was soon turned into sorrow. The servant attempted to carry her, and she, thinking it was somebody that had come to carry her off, as I told her they would, screamed, scratched and bit, till his face was besmeared with blood, and he was glad to put her down. Then she ran to get away from him, and fell down in the streets till her clothes were all besmeared with mud and water. But he kept watch of her, and headed her when he found she was going wrong, until he got her back. And in a sad plight they appeared; she was covered with mud and water, (as it had lately rained, and she had fallen several times in the gutters of the streets,) and he was besmeared with blood. But after she got over her fright, so as to give a history of her adventure, it was amusing indeed. She waited till she found I was asleep, when she crept slyly to the bed, and took some coppers out of my pocket that hung by the head of my bed, and off she started. She went into a number of shops, but she saw no biscuit, neither could she understand a word that any of them said: But she concluded they were all impertinent creatures, and so passed on, till at length she came to a house where she saw the door was open, and the ladies were drinking tea. She went in, and saw biscuit, which was the thing she was after, on the table. She threw down her money upon the table, and took her hand full of biscuit, and went out. The ladies followed her, and came out gabbling round her, *blub, lub, lub, lub*, but she could not tell a word they said. They however filled her bag with biscuit, which was all that she wanted, and she set out for home, feeling as happy as any little creature could well be, until she met the servant before mentioned.

But if the reader has been sufficiently amused with little history, he will now be kind enough to proceed with me in my narrative.

Capt. Mason procured me a passage to Portsmouth, in the Rainbow man-of-war, from whence I was to take passage in a packet for America. Just as I stepped on board the Rainbow, a good lady, with her son, came to make me a visit; her curiosity to see a person of my description was not abated by my being on my passage ; she said she could not sleep till she had seen the person who had suffered such hard fortune. After she had asked all the questions that time would allow of, she gave me a guinea, and half a guinea to my sister, and a muslin handkerchief to each of our little girls. On our arrival at Portsmouth, the packet had sailed ; the captain of the Rainbow, not finding it convenient to keep us with him, introduced us on board the Royal Ann.

Wherever we lived, we found the best friends and the politest treatment. It will be thought singular, that a defenceless woman should suffer so many changes, without meeting some insults, and many incivilities. But, during my long residence on board the various vessels, I received the most delicate attention from my companions. The officers were assiduous in making my situation agreeable, and readily proffered their services.

While on board the Royal Ann, I received the following letters; the reader will excuse the recitation; it would be ingratitude not to record such conspicuous acts of benevolence:—

Plymouth, Sept. 13, 1757.

MADAM:—Late last post night, I received an answer from Mr. Apthorp, who is partner with Mr. Thomlinson, the agent for New Hampshire, with a letter enclosed to you, which gave you liberty to draw on him for fifteen guineas. As Madam Hornech was just closing her letter to you, I gave it her, to enclose for you; I now write again to London on your behalf. You must immediately write Mr. Apthorp what you intend to do, and what further you would have him and our friends at London do for you.

I hope you have received the benefaction of the charitable ladies in this town. All friends here commiserate your misfortunes, and wish you well, together with your sister and children.

Your friend and countryman to serve,
JOHN T. MASON.

Mrs. JOHNSON.

London, Sept. 7, 1757.

MADAM :—I received a letter from Capt. Mason, dated the thirtieth of last month, giving an account of your unfortunate situation, and yesterday Mr. Thomlinson, who is ill, in the country, sent me your letter, together with Capt. Mason's to him, with the papers relative to you. In consequence of which, I this day applied to a number of gentlemen in your behalf, who very readily gave their assistance ; but, as I am a stranger to the steps you intend to pursue, I can only give you liberty, at present, to draw on me for ten or fifteen guineas, for which sum your bill shall be paid, and when you furnish me with information, I shall very cheerfully give any furtherance in my power, to your relief, when I shall also send you a list of your benefactors.

I am, madam,
Your most humble servant,
JOHN APTHORP.

Mrs. SUSANNAH JOHNSON.

LETTER FROM H. GROVE.

"I have now the pleasure to let dear Mrs. Johnson know the goodness of Mrs. Hornech ; she has collected seven pounds for you, and sent it to Mrs. Brett, who lives in the yard at Portsmouth, to beg her favors to you in any thing she can do to help or assist you. She is a good lady ; do go to her, and let her know your distress. Capt. Mason has got a letter, this post, but he is not at home ; cannot tell you further. You will excuse this scrawl, likewise my not enlarging, as Mr. Hornech waits to send it away. Only believe me, madam, you 'have my earnest prayers to God, to help and assist you. My mama's compliments, with mine, and begs to wait on you, and believe me, dear Mrs. Johnson, yours in all events to serve you.

HANNAH GRÒVE.

Sunday Eve, 10 *o'clock.*

I received the donation, and Mr. Apthorp sent me the fifteen guineas. I sincerely lament that he omitted sending me the names of my benefactors.

The captain of the Royal Ann, supposing my situation with him might not be so convenient, applied to the mayor for a permit for me to take lodgings in the city, which was granted. I took new lodgings, where I tarried three or four days, when orders came for me to be on board, the Orange man-of-war in three hours, which was to sail for America. We made all possible despatch, but when we got to the shore, we were astonished to find the ship too far under way to be overtaken. No time was to be lost; I applied to a waterman, to carry us to a merchantman, who was weighing anchor at a distance, to go in the same fleet. He hesitated long enough to pronounce a chapter of oaths, and rowed us off. When we came to the vessel, I petitioned the captain to take us on board, till he overtook the Orange: He directly flew into a violent passion, and offered greater insults than I had ever received during my whole voyage; he swore we were women of bad fame, who wished to follow the army, and that he would have nothing to do with us. I begged him to calm his rage, and we would convince him of his error. But fortunately the victualler of the fleet happened to be

6

in the ship, who at this moment stepped forward
with his roll of names, and told the outrageous
captain that he would soon convince him whether
we deserved notice, by searching his list. He
soon found our names, and the captain began to
beg pardon He took us on board, and apologized
for his rudeness. We sailed with a fair wind
for Cork, where the fleet took provision. We
tarried a fortnight in this place, during which time
the captain of the Orange came on board to see
me, and to offer me a birth in his vessel; but that
being a battle ship, it was thought best for me to
stay where I then was. After weighing anchor at
Cork, we had a passage of seven weeks, remarka-
bly pleasant, to New York. On the tenth of
December, we dropped anchor at Sandy Hook;
on the eleventh, I had the supreme felicity to find
myself on shore in my native country, after an
absence of three years, three months, and eleven
days.

CHAPTER X.

The History ends.

I MIGHT descant for many a page on the felicity
I felt on being once more in my own country;
but others can guess my feelings better than I can
tell them. The mayor of New York ordered
lodgings for us; here I had the pleasure of meeting my friend, Col. Schuler, who gave me much
information about affairs in Canada; he told me
that my husband had been released, and taken
passage in a cartel ship for Halifax, and that he

had redeemed my son from the Indians, for the sum of five hundred livres.

My fellow-prisoner, Labarree, had made his escape from the French, and had been in New York a few days before, on his way home. The reader may reasonably suppose that a more than ordinary friendship might subsist between us, on account of his preserving the life of my infant, and rendering every assistance which it was in his power to perform for us on our journey through the wilderness. Mr. Labarree resided in Charlestown, about two miles from where I lived. We often visited each other after our return, and frequently amused ourselves in the recollection of our journey with the Indians. He amused himself much with my daughter Captive, in her childhood, and was always that benevolent friend through life, which was so peculiarly manifested on the day and journey of our captivity. It so happened, that my daughter was in Charlestown at the time of his last sickness and death. She visited him, and tarried several days, and attended him but only a few days before his death. He often mentioned with satisfaction the peculiar situation of our captivity; little, he said, did he think that he was preserving the life of her in his arms, (speaking of my daughter,) who should be one to attend him in his last days, but that he was happy to have her with him, for she ever appeared to him almost as near as one of his own children. Mr. Labarree was one of those good men who feel for the misfortunes of others. He died August 3d, 1803, aged 79 years.

We tarried in New York ten days, then took water passage for New Haven, where I had the good fortune to find a number of officers, who had been stationed at Charlestown the preceding summer, who gratified my curiosity with intelligence respecting my relations and friends in that place. Some of these gentlemen, among whom was Col. Whiting, kindly undertook to assist us on our journey home, by the way of Springfield. At Hartford we found some gentlemen who were bound for Charlestown; they solicited my sister* to go in company with them, to which she assented.

When within half a dozen miles of Springfield, Mr. Ely, a benevolent friend of Mr. Johnson's, sent his two sons with a sleigh, to convey me to his house, where I proposed staying till some of my friends could hear of my arrival. Fortunately, Mr. Johnson about the same time arrived at Boston, but misfortune had not yet filled the measure of his calamity. He had no sooner landed, than he was put under guard, on suspicion of not performing his duty in the redemption of the Canada prisoners, which suspicion was occasioned by his remissness in producing his vouchers. But the following certificate procured his liberty:—

THIS is to certify, whom it may concern, that the bearer, Lieutenant James Johnson, inhabitant in the town of Charlestown, in the province of New Hampshire, in New England, who, together with his family, were taken by the Indians, on the 30th of August, 1754, has ever since continued a steady and faithful subject to his majesty, King George, and has used his utmost endeavors to re-

* Miss Miriam Willard was afterwards married to the Rev. Mr. Whitney, of Shirley, Massachusetts.

deem his own family, and all others belonging to the province aforesaid, that were in the hands of the French and Indians, which he cannot yet accomplish, and that both himself and family have undergone innumerable hardships and afflictions since they have been prisoners in Canada.

In testimony of which, we the subscribers, officers in his Britannic majesty's service, and now prisoners of war at Quebec, have thought it necessary to grant him this certificate, and do recommend him as an object worthy the aid and compassion of every honest Englishman.

Signed,

PETER SCHUYLER,
ANDREW WATKINS,
WILLIAM MARTIN,
WILLIAM PADGETT.

Quebec, Sept. 16, 1757.

To compensate him for this misfortune, Gov. Pownal recommended a grant, which the general court complied with, and gave him one hundred dollars from the treasury, and he was recorded a faithful subject of King George.

After his dismission from the guards in Boston, he proceeded directly for Charlestown. When within fifteen miles of Springfield, he was met by a gentleman who had just before seen me, who gave him the best news he could have heard; although it was then late at night, he lost not a moment. At two o'clock in the morning of the first of January, 1758, I again embraced my dearest friend. Happy new year! With pleasure would I describe my emotions of joy, could language paint them sufficiently forcible; but the feeble pen shrinks from the task.

Charlestown was still a frontier town, and suffered from savage depredations, which rendered it
an improper residence for me; consequently I
went to Lancaster.

Mr. Johnson in a few days set out for New
York, to adjust his Canada accounts. But on his
journey he was persuaded by Gov. Pownal to take
a captain's commission,* and join the forces bound

* This commission was dated at Boston, the 30th day of
March, in the 31st year of the reign of his majesty, King George
the Second, A.D., 1758, and commissioned him to be a captain
of a company in the battalion of light infantry, to be formed out
of the forces then raised by the governor, for a general invasion
of Canada, commanded by Colonel Oliver Patridge.

When he arrived at Fort Edward, three companies were se-
lected, under the immediate care and command of Maj. Hawks,
and Capt. Johnson was one of them. There were many there
of the soldiers who were acquainted with Capt. Johnson, and
desired to be enrolled in his company, which was complied with.
Deacon Thomas Putnam, now of Charlestown, engaged in his
company as a serjeant, and marched on with him to Ticonderoga,
was with him when the battle began, in which Capt. Johnson
was killed, and gives the following account of the same :—

'On the 8th of July, 1748, Capt. Johnson's company was ordered on the left wing of the army, and we arrived within gun
shot of the breastwork, when the enemy fired upon us. We in
turn fired at them, whenever we had a chance to get sight at
their heads above the breastwork, till we had discharged a dozen
or more shots, at which time the firing appeared to cease on the
part of the enemy. Immediately the enemy hoisted a flag,
which was supposed by Capt. Johnson and others to be a signal
that they were about to give up to our army. A part of his company being still at some distance to the left, Capt. Johnson ordered me to go immediately to the left, to have those cease
firing, saying, with joy, " The day (or battle) is ours." I immediately set out, climbing over brush, trees, and logs, laying
eight or ten feet from the ground. When stepping on a tree,
some rods distance from where I left Capt. Johnson, there was
a full volley fired from the enemy. I escaped from being wounded, a ball only grazing my hat. I let myself down as soon as I
could, and made the best way possible to escape their fire. I
soon found some of my companions that were with Capt. Johnson, who gave me the melancholy tidings of his being shot
through the head, and expired instantly on the spot where I left

for Ticonderoga, where he was killed, on the 8th
of July following, in the battle that proved fatal
to Lord How, while fighting for his country.. Humanity will weep with me. The cup of sorrow
was now replete with bitter drops. All my former
miseries were lost in the affliction of a widow.

In October, 1758, I was informed that my son
Sylvanus was at Northampton, sick of a scald. I
hastened to the place, and found him in a deplorable situation ; he was brought there by Major
Putnam, afterwards Gen. Putnam, with Mrs. How
and her family, who had returned from captivity;
The town of Northampton had taken the charge
of him ; his situation was miserable ; when I
found him, he had no recollection of me, but,
after some conversation, he had some confused
ideas of me, but no remembrance of his father..
It was four years since I had seen him ; he was
then eleven years old. During his absence, he
had entirely forgotten the English language; spoke
a little broken Erench, but was perfect in Indian.
He had been with the savages three years, and
one year with the French. But his habits were
somewhat Indian ; he had been with them in
their hunting excursions, and suffered numerous

him. His body was left on the ground, but his arms and equip-
age, together with some of his clothing, were brought off. I
was acquainted with him from my youth—knew him in the former war, when a lieutenant under the command of Edward Hartwell, Esq., posted at Lunenburg, Townsend, and Narranganset
No. 2, &c. He was universally beloved by his company, and
equally lamented at his death. He was the *soldier's friend*, and
a friend to his country—was of easy manners, pleasant, good
humored, yet strict to obey his orders, and see that those under
his command did the same. The loss to his wife and family was
irreparable ; his acquaintance also lost an agreeable companion,
a valuable member of society, as well as a faithful and valiant
soldier.'

6 *

hardships; he could brandish a tomahawk or bend the bow; but these habits wore off by degrees. I carried him from that place to Lancaster, where he lived a few years with Col. Aaron Willard.

I lived in Lancaster till October, 1759, when I returned to old Charlestown. The sight of my former residence afforded a strange mixture of joy and grief, while the desolations of war, and the loss of a number of dear and valuable friends, combined to give the place an air of melancholy. Soon after my arrival, Major Rogers returned from an expedition against the village St. Francis, which he had destroyed, and killed most of the inhabitants. He brought with him a young Indian prisoner, who stopped at my house; the moment he saw me, he cried, 'My God, my God, here is my sister.' It was my little brother Sabatis, who formerly used to bring the cows for me, when I lived at my Indian masters. He was transported to see me, and declared that he was still my brother, and I must be his sister. Poor fellow! The fortune of war had left him without a single relation; but with his country's enemies he could find one who too sensibly felt his miseries; I felt the purest pleasure in administering to his comfort.

I was extremely fortunate in receiving, by one of Major Rogers's men, a bundle of Mr. Johnson's papers, which he found in pillaging St. Francis. The Indians took them when we were captivated, and they had lain at St. Francis five years.

Sabatis went from Charlestown to Crown Point with Major Rogers. When he got to Otter Creek,

he met my son Sylvanus, who was in the army
with Col. Willard; he recognized him, and clasp-
ing him in his arms. 'My God,' says he; 'the
fortune of war!'—I shall ever remember this
young Indian with affection; he had a high sense
of honor and good behaviour; he was affable,
good natured, and polite.

My daughter Susannah was still in Canada; but
as I had the fullest assurances that every attention was paid to her education and welfare by her
three mothers, I felt less anxiety than I otherwise
might have done.

Every one will imagine that I have paid affliction her utmost demand; the pains of imprison-
ment, the separation from my children, the keen
sorrow occasioned by the death of a butchered
father, and the severe grief arising from my husband's death, will amount to a sum, perhaps unequalled. But still my family must be doomed to
further and severe persecutions from the savages.
In the commencement of the summer of 1760, my
brother-in-law, Mr. Joseph Willard, son of the
Rev. Mr. Willard of Rutland, who was killed by
the Indians in Lovell's war, with his wife and five
children, who lived but two miles distant from
me, were taken by a party of Indians. They were
carried much the same rout that I was to Montreal. Their journey of fourteen days, through
the wilderness, was a series of miseries unknown
to any but those who have suffered Indian captivity; they lost two children, whose deaths were
owing to savage barbarity. The history of their
captivity would almost equal my own; but the
reader's commiseration and pity must now be

exhausted. No more of anguish—no more of sufferings.

They arrived at Montreal a few days before the French surrendered it to the English, and after four months' absence returned home, and brought my daughter Susanna to my arms; while I rejoiced at again meeting my child, whom I had not seen for above five years, I felt extremely grateful to the Misses Jaissons, for the affectionate attention they had bestowed on her. As they had received her as their child, they had made their affluent fortune subservient to her best interest. To give her the accomplishments of a polite education, had been their principal care; she had contracted an ardent love for them, which will never be obliterated. Their parting was an affectionate scene of tears. They never forgot her during their lives; she has eight letters from them, which are proofs of the warmest friendship. My daughter did not know me at her return, and spoke nothing but French; my son spoke Indian, so that my family was a mixture of nations.

Mr. Farnsworth, my only fellow-prisoner whose return I have not mentioned, came home a little before.

Thus, by the goodness of Providence, we all returned, in the course of six painful years, to the place from whence we were taken. The long period of our captivity, and the severity of our sufferings, will be called uncommon and unprecedented. But we even found some friends to pity, among our most persecuting enemies; and, from the various shapes in which mankind appeared, we learned many valuable lessons. Whether in the wilds of Canada, the horrid jails of Quebec, or in

our voyage to Europe, daily occurrences happened, to convince us that the passions of men are as
various as their complexions. And although my
sufferings were often increased by the selfishness
of this world's spirit, yet the numerous testimonies
of generosity I received, bids me suppress the
charge of neglect, or want of benevolence. That
I have been an unfortunate woman, all will grant;
yet my misfortunes, while they enriched my experience, and taught me the value of patience, have
increased my gratitude to the Author of all blessings, whose goodness and mercy have preserved
my life to the present time.

During the time of my widowhood, misfortune
and disappointment were my intimate companions.
In the settlement of my husband's estate, the delay
and perplexity was distressing. I made three
journeys to Portsmouth, fourteen to Boston, and
three to Springfield, to effect the settlement.
Whether my captivity had taught me to be un-
grateful, or whether imagination formed a cata-
logue of evils, I will not pretend to say; but, from
the year 1754 to the present day, greater misfortunes have apparently fallen to my share, than to
mankind in general, and the meteor happiness
has eluded my grasp. The life of a widow is
peculiarly afflictive; but my numerous and long
journies over roads eminently bad, and incidents
that seemed to baffle all my plans and foresight,
render mine more unfortunate than common.

But I found many attentive friends, whose assistance and kindness will always claim my gratitude. Col. White, of Leominster, with whom I
had lived from the time I was eight years old until
1 married, was extremely affectionate and kind;

in his house I found a welcome home. Mr. Samuel Ely, of Springfield, who was the friend of my husband, rendered me numerous kindnesses. Col. Murray, of Rutland, and Col. Chandler, of Worcester, were very friendly and kind. Mr. Clarke, deputy secretary, Gov. Pownall, and Gov. Wentworth, exerted their influence for me in attempting to procure a grant from the general assembly.

In one of my journies to Portsmouth, I conversed with Capt. Adams, who was in Europe at the time I was. He informed me that while there, Mr. Apthorp gave him fourteen pounds sterling, for the purpose of conveying me and my family to America; but my sailing with the convoy prevented my receiving this kindness.

During the four years of my widowhood, I was in quite an unsettled situation; sometimes receiving my children who were returning from captivity, and at others settling the estate of my deceased husband. In October, 1759, I moved to Charlestown, and took possession of my patrimony, consisting of a house, which Col. Whiting had generously assisted my mother in building; in copartnership with my brother, Moses Willard, I kept a small store, which was of service in supporting my family, and settling my husband's estate. I have received, by petitioning, from the general assembly of New Hampshire, forty-two pounds, to indemnify myself and family for losses sustained by our country's enemies. This was of eminent service to me. Mr. Johnson left with Mr. Charles Apthorp, of Boston, the sum which my son's redemption cost, for Col. Schuyler, who had paid the same. But the general assembly of Massachusetts afterwards paid Col. Schuyler his demand for redeeming my son.

By Mr. Johnson I had seven children; two sons and a daughter died in infancy. Sylvanus, with whom the reader is acquainted, now lives in Charlestown. Susanna married Capt. Samuel Wetherbee, and has been the mother of fifteen children, among which were five at two births. Polly married Col. Timothy Bedel, of Haverhill, and died in August, 1789. Captive married Col. George Kimball.

In the year 1762, I married Mr. John Hastings; he was one of the first settlers in Charlestown; I recollect to have seen him when I visited the place in the year 1744; he suffered much by the Indians, and assisted in defending the town during the wars. By him I had seven children; one daughter and four sons died in their infancy. Theodosia is married to Mr. Stephen Hasham. Randilla died at the age of twenty-two; she lived from her infancy with Mr. Samuel Taylor, of Rockingham, by whom she was treated with great affection. I have had thirty-eight grandchildren, and twenty-eight great grandchildren. I lived, till within a few years, on the same spot where the Indians took us from in 1754; but the face of nature has so changed, that old savage fears are all banished.

good and evil, of pleasure and affliction, and I
hope and trust I have profited by the reality, that
others may be profited by the history, which I
leave as a legacy to my friends, as I am now waiting my departure, when I hope to leave the world
in peace. My vacant hours I have often employed
in reflecting on the various scenes that have marked
the different stages of my life. When viewing the
present rising generation, in the bloom of health,
and enjoying those gay pleasures which shed their
exhilerating influence so plentifully in the morn
of life, I look back to my early days, when I too
was happy, and basking in the sunshine of good
fortune. Little do they think, that the meridian
of their lives can possibly be rendered miserable
by captivity or a prison ; as little, too, did I think
that my gilded prospects could be obscured ; but
it was the happy delusion of youth, and I fervent-
ly wish there was no deception. But that Being,
who ' sits upon the circle of the earth, and views
the inhabitants as grasshoppers,' allots our for-
tunes.

Although I have drank so largely from the cup
of sorrow, yet the many happy days I have seen
may be considered as no small compensation.
Twice has my country been ravaged by war since
my remembrance ; I have detailed the share I
bore in the first ; in the last, although the place in
which I lived was not a field of bloody battle, yet
its vicinity to Ticonderoga, and the savages that
ravaged the Coos country, rendered it perilous and
distressing. But now no one can set a higher
value on the smiles of peace than myself. The
savages are driven beyond the lakes, and our
country has no enemies. The gloomy wilderness,

6 †

that fifty years ago secreted the Indian and the beast of prey, has vanished away, and the thrifty farm smiles in its stead. The Sundays, that were then employed in guarding a fort, are now quietly devoted to worship. The tomahawk and scalping-knife have given place to the ploughshare and sickle, and prosperous husbandry now thrives where the terrors of death once chilled us with fear.

My numerous progeny have often gathered around me, to hear the sufferings once felt by their aunt or gradmother, and wonder at their magnitude.

My daughter Captive still keeps the dress she appeared in when brought to my bedside by the French nurse, at the Ticonderoga hospital, and often refreshes my memory with past scenes, when showing it to her children. These things yield a kind of melancholy pleasure.

Perhaps the reader's patience is by this time exhausted, and I shall not detain him much longer; but I cannot dismiss the subject without making mention of some occurrences which have taken place since the first edition of my narrative was published.

In the year 1798, my daughter Captive and family removed to the province of Lower Canada, which was no small grief to me. For the space of forty years and upwards, we were together on the anniversary day of her birth, which was a great consolation to me in my declining years. And even after she was gone, although the distance was nearly two hundred miles, that anniversary day never passed unthought of or unnoticed by me, and I presume it never did by her, as she has often informed me since her return. The extraordinary occurrences of God's providence, in preserving our lives through the various scenes which we passed in her infancy and childhood, might reasonably be supposed to attach that parental and dutiful affection to each other, which could only be extinguished by the extinction of life.

My life, in many other respects, has been a scene of trouble and misfortune, since I published my narrative in 1796. Some time in October, in 1801, I had been on a visit to Mr. Samuel Taylor's, in Rockingham; on my return, accompanied by his daughter, at the south end of the street in Charlestown, our horse was started by a boy wheeling a load of flax, which threw me from the horse. The violence of the fall was so great, together with a wound cut deep in my forehead, that I was taken up for dead, or apparently senseless, by my grandson, Jason Wetherbee, and carried to the house of Samuel Stevens, Esq., about thirty rods. Every aid and assistance possible was made for me. After my revival, the wounds were dressed; the cut was sewed up by Mrs. Page, the wife of Capt. Peter Page, of Charlestown. In a short time, I so far recovered as to be removed to my home, which was nearly one mile. I recovered my former strength as soon as might be expected, considering the badness of the wound and bruises which I received by the fall.

My husband, Mr. John Hastings, with my consent and agreement, had, prior to this time, given our estate to Mr. Stephen Hasham, who married our only daughter; in consequence of which, my life and living were so immediately under his con troul, that my situation was rendered very unhappy. But a respect for the feelings of the surviving relatives will prevent my going into a detail of my sufferings, while under Mr. Hasham's roof—which, considering the different treatment I had a right to expect, under the care and protection of a son-in-law, I sometimes found almost as painful to be borne as my savage captivity.

In the spring of 1803, my daughter Captive came from Canada, with a sick daughter of hers, to be doctored, as physicians were at a great distance from where she resided. In the summer, I made known to her my unhappy situation, as did my husband also. She, by the consent of my husband, and the advice of some respectable friends, procured a home for me at Mr. Jonathan Baker's, whose wife was daughter to my daughter Wetherbee, where I resided till February following, when, with the assistance of Mr. Kimball and his brother, who was in company with him on his journey to remove his wife and daughter to Canada, I was conveyed to Concord, in Vermont, to Mr. Wetherbee's, my son-in-law, where I remained about ten months. We had intelligence, in the early part of November, that my husband was very sick; but the season and badness of the roads prevented my immediate return to see him. He died on the 21st day of November, 1804, in the ——— year of his age.

In the January following, I came to Charlestown, when, by the assistance of Mr. Wetherbee and others, I concluded a settlement with Mr. Hasham, in which I received the rents of certain pieces of land yearly, to continue during my natural life, which is sufficient to support me comfortably, and I can expend it where I please. I made my principal residence at Mrs. Rice's, who is a niece of mine, and sometimes with Mr. Wetherbee, my grandson, and visited my other relations, and was in as good health as might be expected for a person of my years.

I would here gladly close my narrative, but I have one more sad event to detail. In March, 1808, Mr. Kimball and family returned from Canada, and made their residence in Langdon, adjoining Charlestown, to which place I removed to reside with them, where I enjoyed myself happily, with my daughter Captive and her family, for about eighteen months—sometimes making visits among my many relatives and acquaintances, as it was convenient. In October, 1809, for to make it more convenient for Mr. Kimball to carry on his mechanical business, I concluded to make a short visit to Charlestown, to spend the winter at my old quarters, with Mrs. Rice. Accordingly, on the 14th of October, I set out for that purpose, in company with Mr. Kimball and Mr. John Sartwell, in whose waggon we all rode. We had not proceeded far from Mr. Sartwell's house, when, descending down a small pitch in the road, the staple drew out of the yoke, and let the spire drop, and the waggon pushing upon the horses, and striking their heels, soon set them out upon the run. The waggon, by some means or other, immediately upset, and came completely bottom up—so suddenly, also, that it caught all three of us under it. In the situation, we were dragged, as nearly as could be ascertained afterwards by the blood, about six rods, when, by some cause or other, the waggon hoisted so as to let us out from under it. The horses soon 'cleared themselves from the waggon, and run about a half a mile. We were all, as must be expected, very much hurt. Mr. Sartwell had no bones broke, but was very much bruised, so that he was confined for some time. Mr. Kimball had one shoulder dislocated, and two fingers taken off from his left hand, besides being otherwise bruised. He can now use only his thumb and little finger of his left hand, the finger next to the little one being stiff. I had one ancle broken, and the bone very much shattered, besides being otherwise bruised. I was carried back on a bier to my son Kimball's, where we both lay several weeks, and endured much excruciating pain. When I was laid on the bier to be carried back, it brought fresh to my mind the bier that the Indians made for me after the birth of my daughter Captive. It was thought by many, and I was even apprehensive myself, that the pain I endured, together with my age, would have proved too hard for me. But, by the blessing of God, my life is still preserved, and I am once more restored to as comfortable a measure of health as I can expect with my years.* I am now in the winter of life, and feel sensibly the effects of old age. I have removed back to Charlestown, as also my daughter Captive, and

* 'Tis with satisfaction, that I here express my unfeigned thanks to Dr. Kitteridge and Dr. Carpenter, for their particular attention to me during my confinement; also to the Rev. A. Kneeland, for his prayers, and frequent visits during the same. It also gives me much satisfaction in reflecting, (although my pains were almost intolerable,) that my daughter Captive was able to attend me, which she did with her wonted cheerfulness, although many times I was fearful it might prove too hard for her health and constitution.

7

her family. It is a matter of great consolation to me, that I have it in my power to spend so much of my time with her in my latter days. I have had many a sorrowful hour on her account, in her infancy and childhood, and she has richly repaid them in her tender affection to me in my eve of life.

Instances of longevity are remarkable in my family. My aged mother, before her death, could say to me, arise, daughter, and go to thy daughter; for thy daughter's daughter has got a daughter; a command which few mothers can make and be obeyed.

And now, kind reader, after sincerely wishing that your days may be as happy as mine have been unfortunate, I bid you adieu.

Charlestown, September 10, 1810.

Note.—Mrs. Johnson died in November, 1810, soon after the close of the foregoing narrative.

APPENDIX.

THE subject of the foregoing narrative lived but a short time after the last date. She was very anxious to have this work revised and republished before her death. She had several conversations with me on the subject, while she lived in Langdon, and wished me to undertake the work, and get the copy-right secured to her daughter Captive, (Mrs. Kimball,) which I told her I would do, if time and opportunity would permit. But the sad accident and misfortune she met with soon after, as has been mentioned, together with other circumstances, prevented its being done at that time. I was in Charlestown, Mass., at the time of her death, and on my return home, was informed by Col. Kimball, that it was the earnest desire of the old lady, in her last sickness, that I should attend her funeral, and preach a sermon on the occasion; which sermon she wished to have annexed to her narrative, as I had undertaken to revise the copy, and had not completed it. My being absent at the time of her death prevented the compliance with her request. But, that I might in some measure comply with her wishes, and being particularly solicited by Col. Kimball, whose wife is the daughter Captive, so often mentioned in the narrative, I preached a sermon on their account, at Langdon, on the 10th of February, 1811, and have annexed the substance of it to the narrative, by way of appendix.

A sermon is also added, which was preached by the Rev. Dan Foster, late of Charlestown, at the funeral of Mrs. Whitcomb, formerly Mrs. Willard, the mother of Mrs. Johnson, *alias* Mrs. Hastings, the subject of this narrative.

I would further remark, that this narrative has been considerably enlarged, from papers furnished me by Col. Kimball, together with what I had pre-viously taken from Mrs. Hastings' own mouth, and also the circumstance of the accident which happened at Langdon, which I was knowing to myself, and I believe the whole to be a correct statement of facts.

ABNER KNEELAND.

Langdon, Sept. 18, 1811.

A SERMON,

*Occasioned by the Death of Mrs. Hastings, who died Nov. 27th, 1810, in the eighty-first year of her age.**

' But if a man live many years, and rejoice in them all ; yet let him remember the days of darkness, for they are many.'—ECCL. xi. 8.

IT will be proper just to premise, that the occasion of reading these words at this time, is the late death of the aged and honorable Mrs. Hastings, a person with whom many of you, my hearers, have been long acquainted; and many more, if not all, have been made familiar with the narrative of her captivity and unparalleled sufferings ; and your feeling sensibility has often been excited with the perusal or recital of those trying scenes through which she was called to pass, in the first settlement of this country.

To dilate, therefore, on her life or character, would be useless at this time (as it would be nothing new) to you who are present, and if this discourse should ever be more extensively known, the most essential and important parts of her life will go with it. And as she has bid the world adieu, and the most solemn scene of her funeral is already past, it will not so much be expected that I should enter into those particulars at this time. Suffice it, therefore, to say, that, having lived to a good

* She breathed out her last expiring moments, till life was extinct, supported in the arms of her daughter Captive, for whom she ever manifested the greatest affection.

old age—having experienced many of the various dispensations of the providence of God—in prosperity and in adversity—in joy and in sorrow—she has at last resigned her worn-out life, with a firm hope of a future immortality.

Happy, indeed, should I have been, to have complied with her wishes, so far as to have attended her interment, and delivered this discourse to her surrounding relations and friends, who attended on the solemn occasion. But as my absence at the time prevented it, we shall now dispense with any addresses that might then have been thought proper, and shall only attend to a doctrinal disquisition of the text.

'But if a man live many years, and rejoice in them all; yet let him remember the days of darkness, for they are many.'

The mortality of man is such, that but a very few, comparatively speaking, live to what is called *old age.* There are so many casualties incident to human nature, that the prospect of living 'many years' is rendered doubtful, and very uncertain. By an attention to the bills of mortality, it will be seen that the number who arrive to three score years and ten (what is called the common age of man) is but very small in comparison with the whole that are born; and although some, by reason of strength, live to four score years and upwards, yet is that strength, labor and sorrow; for it is soon cut off, and we fly away.

Virtue itself does not shield a man against the natural evils incident to human life. And, though some may seem to have more of a full share than others, yet no one ought to expect wholly to avoid them.

We are not, however, to estimate a man's moral character by what outwardly befalls him, because time and chance must happen to all men ; and, if we wish to learn the real character of a man, we must notice with what patience, with what fortitude and resignation, he endures the adverse scenes of life, and likewise his faithfulness in performing his duty, though in the midst of peril and danger.

Passing over the uncertainty of human life, which is apparent to all, I shall notice but two propositions from the text, and show,

I. What is necessary to enable a man to rejoice in all his days, and

II. That the sorrows and afflictions incident to human nature are not incompatible with the joys of a Christian.

I. What is necessary to enable a man to rejoice in all his days ?

1st, In order to pass through life comfortably and happy, and rejoice in all the dispensations of the providence of God, it is necessary that we should be made to know that 'all things work *together for good*,' though manifested only 'to them that love God—to them that are called according to his purpose'—that the knowledge, the wisdom, the power, and even the love or goodness of God, extends to all events, even to the most minute circumstances in his providential dealings with the children of men —that no event can take place without his divine permission, and that what he permits, all circumstances considered, is best so to be—that there is no calculating upon any thing in this lower world as being certain to us, but *death*, and even *that*, the time when is uncertain—that, through the

5 *

weakness of our understanding, the short-sighted-
ness of our knowledge, (every thing we see being
temporal,) although the order of things is unalter-
ably fixed in the eternal mind, yet to us they are
mutable, and therefore liable to change. And, if
we have been enabled to extend our thoughts so
far as to discover the immutability of things in
God, it is necessary that we should know that
they are immutably *good;* for how can a rational
being rejoice in an unalterable evil? And, furthermore, it increases our felicity, to know that
all things are not only established for good, but
that they are established on rational principles—
not by a blind chance, not simply by an unavoid-
able fate—for even good conferred upon us, upon
such principles, would not excite our gratitude to
God, any more than a prize-ticket, drawn to us,
would excite our gratitude to the managers of the
lottery; but the good which we receive is established by God himself, as being the fruits of infinite wisdom, effected by unlimited power, and
prompted by unbounded love or goodness. And,
if we are rationally convinced that all events are
wisely determined, it does not militate against our
peace or happiness, to suppose that the providence
of God respecting them is immutably and unal-
terably established. For, when any thing is once
ordered for the *best*, it cannot be altered for the
better, because there is nothing better than the
best.

That the foreknowledge of God extends to all
events, and that he overrules, superintends, and
governs all events, are truths that will not be dis-
puted or denied by any who believe in a Supreme
Being. And, if we acknowledge that God governs

all events, we must acknowledge that he governs them all for the best, or else we must acknowledge that he governs all events, but not, or at least not *all* of them, for the best; which idea would be blasphemously absurd.

The Pharisees, when Christ was here in the flesh, were reminded by him of their blasphemy, when, because they could not. deny the miracles which he wrought, they accused him of having an unclean spirit, and that he cast out devils through Beelzebub, the prince of the devils. And the idea that God does, or ever will punish his creatures, but not for their *good*, is equally derogatory of his character. Such ideas do not become the faithful child of God. He rejoices that God overrules and superintends all events, and that, however grievous they may be to be borne, they are wisely calculated to yield the peaceable fruits of righteousness to them that are exercised thereby.

This is the Christian's consolation. Such faith as this is able to solace the deepest affliction, and give patience and fortitude to the mind. It strengthens the understanding, and gives vigilance to the animal faculties, so as to enable us to go through any pain, peril, or danger; when prudentially deemed expedient, to preserve our own lives or the lives of others. A firm confidence in God is therefore absolutely necessary, to enable us to rejoice, or even calmly to acquiesce, in the dispensations of his providence.

2d, A constant and inflexible adherence to the principles of virtue is also absolutely necessary, to enable us to rejoice in all our days.

That a deviation from this principle should produce guilt, pain, condemnation, horror, and remorse, appears to be one of the unalterable laws of moral nature. In vain may a man attempt to assuage his guilt, or calm his conscience, with the idea that *he could not have done otherwise,* when he intends to do, or in fact has done, that which his own conscience tells him is wrong. For his guilt, and all the evil consequences that follow, are as morally certain as his crime. The carnal mind always reasons, if he attempts to reason at all, contrary to facts and our daily experience. He would willingly admit the moral certainty of all events, if he could thereby exculpate himself from *blame.* And of course the carnal mind will argue thus—that he was under the fatal necessity of doing as he did; hence, the blame, if any there be, cannot be in the creature. Not realizing that *guilt,* and all the evil consequences of sin, are as much *events* in the providence of God, as the *crimes* that produce them—and it being consistent with infinite wisdom and goodness to suffer, permit, or allow, sin to exist in the moral system, certainly it cannot be inconsistent with the same wisdom and goodness, even to *decree* that guilt and misery should be its direful consequences. For one, I am so fully convinced that virtue produces its own reward, and sin carries with it its own punishment, that I will venture to give it as a maxim, which I believe will ever hold true, that whatsoever produces no guilt, no shame, no remorse, no condemnation, in a word, no evil consequences, even to the sinner himself, is not sin. It may, however, be stated here, by way of objection, that a man may wrong his neighbor, or friend, without producing any injury to himself, and that such an act is sin. I grant that it is sin for any one man, knowingly, to injure another, or to give unjust or unnecessary pain, even to an enemy; but I deny the possibility of his doing it without producing the greatest injury to himself; and such a proposition ought to be first proved before it is taken for granted. One man may be the occasion of disturbing the peace of many; but he never can, by his own act, be the cause of the guilt of any but himself. It is true he may, by his evil example, induce others to commit the same crime, and thereby become equally guilty; but they are not guilty till they follow the evil example. And my hearers will be capable of judging which is the greatest misery—*sorrow* occasioned by the evil conduct of others, or *guilt* produced by our own crimes. My conscience tells me that the latter is the most to be dreaded.

My maxim is equally good on the side of virtue. That which produces no peace, no comfort, no consolation, in a word, no good consequences, even to the *doer* of the deed, is not virtue. And furthermore, whoever bestows a favor on another, is the greatest partaker of the benefit, because ' *it is more blessed to give than to receive.*' If 'this sentiment be correct, as I presume it is; how blessed, indeed, must be our heavenly Father, who is the giver and bestower of every good and perfect gift, both spiritual and temporal! And how miserable indeed must be the condition of that man who is entirely destitute of a principle of benevolence! Whoever, therefore, would see good days, and rejoice in them all, must adhere to the strictest observance of virtue. All outward professions, without this internal principle, are but a mere name, as empty in its sound as the

' sounding brass or the tinkling cymbal.' He, and he only, let him live many years or few, that keepeth a conscience void of offence towards God and man, may be truly said to rejoice in all his days.

- 3d, Hope in immortality is also necessary, to enable a man to rejoice in all his days.

Short of this hope, the best prospects in life are but an awful uncertainty. One thought of death blasts all our expectations in this life, as it respects ourselves, and a gloomy, dismal, and uncertain hereafter, is the only refuge to all those who have not a well-grounded hope in immortality.

This hope is obtained only by a firm belief in the religion of Jesus Christ. In him, life and immortality are brought to light through the gospel. And whoever can fully believe, (and whoever feels interested enough to examine the testimony will not doubt of the fact,) that God raised up Jesus from the dead, can, from the same source of evidence, easily believe that the same power will raise up *us* also, and make us sit together with him, in heavenly places. ' For if God spared not his own Son, but delivered him up for us all, how shall he not also with him freely give us all things ?'—' who hath blessed us with all spiritual blessings, according as he hath chosen us in him, before the foundation of the world, that we should be holy and without blame before him in love.' ' Whoever hath this hope in him, (i. e., in Christ,) will purify himself even as he is pure.' And from the purity of his life and conduct he will be enabled to rejoice in all his days.

When we can, amidst all the trials, losses, crosses, affliction, and disappointments, incident to human life, look, by an eye of faith, beyond all death and time, into that spiritual world, where sorrow can never come, and there, through the testimony of the mouth of God's holy prophets, behold the 'ransomed of the Lord returning, and coming to him with songs and everlasting joys upon their heads, where they shall obtain joy and gladness, and sorrow and sighing shall flee away,' and, through the fulness of the gospel, believe that Christ 'gave himself a ransom for all, to be testified in due time,' will view all such afflictions but momentary, and therefore will receive them as specimens of the wisdom and goodness of our heavenly Father, being calculated to work out for us 'a far more exceeding and eternal weight of glory.' Hence every bitter has its sweet—every sorrow is tempered with the spirit of consolation; and we have every reason to believe, that, as our day is, so will our strength be, and that, while we are destined to live in this world, God will lay no more upon us than what he will enable us to bear. All pain must be either tolerable or intolerable; if tolerable, it may be endured; but if intolerable, it must be short; for the moment that pain becomes intolerable, it destroys all sense, and therefore ceases to be pain.

Such faith, such hope, and such confidence in God, will be sufficient to bear up the soul under all trials, carry it through all difficulties, giving it the final victory over sin and death.

4th, As all mankind have sinned, and come short of the glory of God, in order for us to get the victory over the sting of death, which is sin, it is necessary that we should know that 'God is in Christ reconciling the world unto himself, not

7 †

imputing unto them their trespasses, but hath
made him to be sin (or rather a sin-offering) for
us, who knew no sin, that we might be made the
righteousness of God in him.' And, as repentance and remission of sins are necessary to
reconciliation, God hath exalted Jesus to be 'a
Prince and a Savior, to give repentance unto
Israel, and remission of sins.' And is he the God
of the Jews only? Is he not the God of the
Gentiles also? Yes, of the Gentiles also. For
God, who is rich in mercy, hath 'concluded them
all in unbelief, that he might have mercy upon all.'
A remission, therefore, of all our sins that are
past, and a salvation from sin for the future, is
also necessary, to enable us to rejoice in all our
days. This brings me to show,

II. That the sorrows and afflictions incident
to human nature are not incompatible with the
joys of a Christian.

'Although affliction cometh not forth of the
dust, neither doth trouble spring out of the ground,
yet man is born unto trouble, as the sparks fly
upward.' And although some are called to pass
through much greater scenes of sorrow and affliction than others, yet there are none wholly exempt. In this respect, 'time and chance happen
unto all men.' 'All things come alike to all.
There is one event to the righteous and to the
wicked; to the good, and to the clean, and to the
unclean; to him that sacrificeth, and to him that
sacrificeth not.' Virtue, morality, religion, yea,
even piety itself, does not exempt mankind from
any natural evil to which we are subject. Neither
is sin certain to produce any of those misfortunes
to which we are always liable by the providence

of God. If, therefore, there be no certain and necessary connexion between virtue and prosperity, in the things of this world, and sin and adversity, or the misfortunes of life, then there is nothing that necessarily debars us from partaking of all the joys of a Christian, notwithstanding our temporal life may be a scene of sorrow aud affliction.

The original organization and constitution of the human body is sufficient to convince any rational mind, that is not fettered with the prejudices of a false education, that these bodies were never designed for an immortal state; for 'flesh and blood cannot inherit the kingdom of God, neither can corruption inherit incorruption.' Mortality is instamped upon all animated nature; and man, in this respect, hath no pre-eminence above a beast. 'For that which befalleth the sons of men befalleth beasts; even one thing befalleth them: as the one dieth, so dieth the other; yea, they have all one breath.'*. Has sin affected the brutal creation, and produced their mortality? or was man mortal, and subject to death even before sin entered the moral system? It is true, it was not revealed unto Adam, that he was dust, and must return to the dust again, till after the transgression; but it was as true before as it was afterwards; for the Lord God *formed man of the dust of the ground*—gave him an earthly constitution, which was sensual, corruptible, yea, mortal. The evils of mortality, therefore, ought not to be imputed to sin. I am willing to grant that the miseries of this mortal state may be greatly increased

* Eccl. iii. 10.

by sin. But what I would wish to be understood to say, is, that the seeds of mortality were sown in man in the original constitution of his nature, and that he was ever, after being formed of the dust, subject to natural death, and must have experienced the natural evils attendant on this life, such as pains, sickness, providential misfortunes, and even natural death, if man had never sinned.

Again. It is said of Jesus, that 'he shall save his people from their sins.' And, if he will save them from their sins, it is most rational to believe, that by so doing he will save them from all the consequences of sin. But Christ has never yet saved, and we have no reason to expect that he ever will save, a soul from natural death.

Christ himself, although without sin, was subject to natural death. Death reigned from Adam to Moses, even on those who had not shined after the similitude of Adam's transgression. And death still is, and ever has been, the common lot of all animated nature, Enoch and Elijah excepted. And I should consider those two instances as early intimations of an immortal state, rather than an evidence that man originally was not subject to natural death.

Much more might be said, to establish this proposition, if it were necessary; but our argument does not rest wholly on this particular point; for, even should we admit that natural, as well as moral death, is the effect of sin, yet, when we reflect that we have an advocate with the Father, even Jesus Christ the righteous, 'who gave himself a propitiation for our sins, and not for ours only, but for the sins of the whole world,' we can anticipate the time when all the consequences of sin, whether natural or moral, will be completely at an end, and death swallowed up of life.

Such a remembrance of the *days of darkness* as this, will serve to sweeten all our enjoyments, and give a zest to every real pleasure. We should remember the evil days only to enhance our joys at the sight of deliverance, to brighten our hopes in the prospect of future glory, and to excite our gratitude for the unmerited blessing. And such considerations should further serve to give us fortitude of mind to endure providential evils with patience and resignation while they continue.

The sentiments inculcated in this discourse have been completely verified in the thoroughly-tried life and unshaken death of her who has been the occasion of it. She has gone down to the dust in a good old age, like a shock of corn, fully ripe, richly laden with the experience of the goodness of God. Her fortitude has been remarkable ; and to this, under the providence of God, perhaps, may be imputed, the preservation of her life through scenes the most unparalleled of which history affords. Where one would have survived, it is more than probable that hundreds would have suffered death under more favorable circumstances.

Her sufferings have been so great, that many who have read her narrative have believed the whole to be a fiction—a mere idle tale, published to amuse the credulous part of community, and get their money. But the additional circumstances in the latter part of her life, together with her death, will give new strength to the evidence, and make her narrative still more interesting. The plain, simple facts were sufficiently interesting, not to need the imagination of the poet, or the eloquence of the orator, to engage the attention of every feeling heart.

The last respects to her remains have been paid. She has paid the last debt of nature, which we must all pay sooner or later—an affecting stroke, to be sure, to her surviving children and friends, though nothing more than what they have long had reason to expect. After surviving so many trying scenes, from all of which she had recovered, she calmly resigned her life, apparently being worn out with old age. You have, therefore, my respected friends, no serious cause to mourn; but rather may you rejoice, that, the earthly house of her tabernacle being dissolved, you have every reason to believe that she hath a building of God, an house not made with hands, eternal in the heavens.

She is gone to the world of spirits, and thither must we all follow her sooner or later. 'For the dust must return to the earth as it was, but the spirit to God who gave it.' May we all so live, and so conduct, whilst the brittle thread of life is lengthened out unto us, and also may we possess that faith, hope, and confidence in our God, that, when he shall call us, to bid adieu to the things of time and sense, we may go on our way rejoicing—be enabled to look back on our past lives, with the pleasing satisfaction, that we kept a conscience void of offence toward God and toward man. Having our work done, and well done, which was alotted us here to do, may we have nothing to do but to die—calmly falling asleep in Jesus Christ; may we close our eyes in peace on all sublunary enjoyments—rest in hope, till we shall arise to a glorious immortality—be clothed upon with our house from above, and be received into those realms of celestial glory, where no sin nor sorrow shall ever enter; there may our hearts be tuned upon the golden lyre of God's grace, to join with seraphs and angels, and all the beatified spirits of the ransomed of the Lord, which shall compose the heavenly hosts, to celebrate the praises of him who is worthy to receive all possible glory, honor, and power, throughout an ever-beginning, and never-ending eternity. Which may God grant to be the happy lot and portion of all the ransomed sons and daughters of Adam, for the sake of the 'Mediator between God and men, the man Christ Jesus, who gave himself a *ransom* for all, to be testified in due time, to whom, with God, the Father of our Lord Jesus Christ, 'who hath blessed us with spiritual blessings,' be ascribed all honor and glory, now, henceforth, and forever more. Amen.

8

THE BURIAL OF A MOTHER.

BEHOLD the sad impending stroke,
 Which now arrests our eyes;
The silken bands of union broke—
 A tender mother dies!

She's gone! she's gone to realms above,
 Where saints and angels meet,
To realize her Savior's love,
 And worship at his feet.

Her pains and groans are now all o'er;
 She's gone to God on high;
Her wishful eyes shall weep no more—
 No more her spirit sigh.

For you who round her body mourn,
 And drop the flowing tears,
How many sorrows she hath borne,
 In all her lengthened years!

Her sorrows now are at an end;
 The Lord did for her call,
And Jesus is her only friend,
 Her life, her health, her ALL.

A SERMON,

*Delivered at the Funeral of Mrs. Whitcomb, May 7th, 1797.—*By DAN FOSTER, A.M.

'But thanks be to God, who giveth us the victory, through our Lord Jesus Christ.'—1 COR. xv. 57.

WERE it not for the hope of eternal life, given us in Christ Jesus, the departure of near friends and relatives, and the thoughts of death, would be accompanied with sorrows almost insupportable. To be as though we never had been, at best, is but a gloomy thought ; but an eternal existence in sin and misery, is a thought infinitely more intolerable. Any thing short, then, of possessing the hope of life and immortality, promised in the gospel, would render all beyond the grave, at best, but a sad and awful uncertainty. And although the Christian has no positive demonstration, as it is necessary, whilst he tabernacles in the flesh, that he should walk 'by faith, and not by sight;' yet, relying on the divine testimony, he possesses a hope that is like an 'anchor to his soul, both sure and stedfast ;' which hope entereth into that within the vail, where Jesus, our propitiation and forerunner hath entered for us. This hope giveth us the victory, and enables us to triumph over the fear of death. I shall proceed, on this occasion, in the following order :—

I. I will endeavor to state the connexion of the words with the context, and show the general instruction contained in the chapter, and,

II. Make a practical use of the meaning of the text.

In the beginning of the chapter, the apostle refers to the gospel which he had preached, and speaks of its nature and importance, as in ver. 1—4. 'Moreover, brethren, I declare unto you the gospel which I preached unto you, which also ye have received, and wherein ye stand ; by which also ye are saved, if ye keep in memory what I preached unto you, unless ye have believed in vain. For I delivered unto you, first of all, that which I also received, how that Christ died for our sins, according to the scriptures, and that he was buried, and that he rose again the third day, according to the scriptures.' Hence it is evident the doctrine of the resurrection of the dead, was contained in the gospel of Jesus Christ, which Paul preached. Yea, the knowledge of salvation, the knowledge of God, whom to know is life eternal, comes to man through the medium of the gospel, which is 'good tidings of great joy to all people.'

Some of the most important articles of the gospel, which is our salvation, are these :—that 'Christ died for our sins ;' i. e., to procure the remission of them, to propitiate them, and reconcile us to God, 'according to the scriptures.' As the apostle observes, ' If any man sin, we have an advocate with the Father, Jesus Christ the righteous; and he is the propitiation for our sins, and not for ours only, but also for the sins of the whole world.' ' For the love of Christ constraineth us, because we thus judge, that if one died for all, then were all dead ; and he died for all, that they who live should not live unto themselves, but unto

him that died for them and rose again.' Isaiah
gives us the same idea of the design of the death
of Christ : see chap. liii. ver. 5, 6. '.But he was
wounded for our transgressions ; he was bruised
for our iniquities ; the chastisement of our peace
was upon him ; and with his stripes we are healed.
All we, like sheep, have gone astray ; we have
turned every one to his own way ; and the Lord
hath laid on him the iniquity of us all.'

We are not only taught by the scriptures, that
Christ died for our sins, but that he rose again for
our justification, as the apostle elsewhere observes :
—'Who was delivered for our offences, and rose
again for our justification ; therefore, being justified by faith, we have peace with God, through
our Lord Jesus Christ ; by whom also we have
access by faith in this grace' wherein we stand,
and rejoice in hope of the glory of God.' In consequence of the resurrection of Christ, the apostle,
and we, and all believers, are *justified* in having
faith in him as a divine person, the Messias of
whom Moses and the prophets did write—the Shi-
loh, who was to come ; the Just One, to whom the
gathering of the people shall be ; the Lamb of God,
who taketh away the sin of the world ; the Christ,
who, by the blood of his cross, shall reconcile all
things unto himself; the Savior, who shall save
his people from their sins ; the Mediator, who
gave himself a ransom for all, to be testified in
due time. The apostle speaks of the resurrection
of Christ, as a matter of vast importance, and as
a thing, of sufficient certainty. See the importance attached to the resurrection of Christ by the
apostle, as expressed in the 17th verse of the con-

text:—'And if Christ be not raised, your faith is vain ; ye are yet in your sins.'

If Christ arose not from the dead, we have no reason to confide in him as a divine person, the Messias, the Mediator with God, the Captain of our salvation; and we have no reason to expect reconciliation to God through him ; yea, we can have no hope in the resurrection of the dead ; for the apostle expressly says, 'If the dead rise not, then is not Christ raised.' And, according to the apostle's mode of reasoning, (who was a good reasoner,) if Christ be not raised, then will the dead rise not, agreeably to the 18th verse :—'Then they also which are fallen asleep in Christ are perished.' But the apostle turns his hypothetical mode of reasoning into affirmative and positive assertions, as in verse 20th, and on :—'But now is Christ risen from the dead, and become the first fruits of them that slept. For since by man came death, by man came also the resurrection of the dead. For as in Adam all die, even so in Christ shall all be made alive. But every man in his own order: Christ the first fruits: afterward they that are Christ's at his coming. Then cometh the end, when he shall have delivered up the kingdom to God, even the Father ; when he shall have put down all rule, and all authority and power. For he must reign, till he hath put all enemies under his feet. The last enemy that shall be destroyed is death.' Thus we may see the importance attached to the death of Christ.

And the certainty of his triumphing over death, and reascending to his native heaven, cannot be reasonably doubted, when we consider that he was actually seen alive, after his crucifixion, by many creditable witnesses. He was seen of Cephas, of the twelve, and afterwards of above five hundred at once; some of whom were 'fallen asleep, but many remained when Paul wrote the above testimony. And last of all he was seen of the apostle, who, in all his writings, and in the whole history of his life, appears to have been a man of good abilities, considerable literature, and of a sound, strong mind, not addicted to enthusiastic flights, but in all his reasoning appealing to incontestible facts, as the foundation of his arguments, which he knew were incontrovertible, and must be acknowledged by his opponents.

Another important article of the gospel of our salvation, is, that human bodies shall rise again. ' This corruptible shall put on incorruption, and this mortal shall put on immortality.' ' For we are not appointed unto wrath, but to obtain salvation.' So we see that man is appointed to obtain salvation through Jesus Christ. See verse 19th of the context :—' If in this life only we have hope in Christ, we are of all men the most miserable.' See also the 20th verse, and on, before quoted. How glorious a discovery this ! What a display of gospel grace ! This mortal shall put on immortality ! That which is sown in weakness shall be raised in power ! That which is sown a natural body shall be raised a spiritual body ! That which is sown in dishonor shall be raised in glory !

Another most important article of the gospel which St. Paul preached, is this, that Jesus, the Son of God, the Savior of the world, shall sway the mediatorial sceptre, till all the enemies of the moral administration of Jehovah shall be subdued, and brought into voluntary, cheerful subjection.

8 *

'For he,' that is, Christ, 'must reign, till he hath
put all enemies under his feet. The last enemy
that shall be destroyed is death. For he,' that is,
God supreme, God the Father of all, 'hath put
all things under his,' that is, under Christ, the
Son's, 'feet. But when he saith, All things are
put under him, it is manifest that he,' the Father,
'is excepted, which did put all things under him,'
the Son. 'And when all things shall be subdued
unto him,' the Son, 'then shall the Son also himself be subject,' made like unto his brethren, 'unto
HIM that put all things under *him*, that God may
be all in all.'

The apostle then proceeds to state, what has
been before noticed, the surprising transformation
of human bodies at the resurrection. See verses
42, 44. 'So also is the resurrection of the dead;
it is sown in corruption, it is raised in incorruption;
it is sown in dishonor, it is raised in glory; it is
sown in weakness, it is raised in power; it is sown
a natural body, it is raised a spiritual body.'

O how great, how glorious will this change be,
of our poor, frail, mortal bodies!

The apostle next proceeds to speak of the
change which living men shall experience, when
Christ shall come again, and the celestial trumpet
shall raise the dead. See ver. 51—53:—'Behold,
I show you a mystery. We shall not all sleep,
but shall all be changed, in a moment, in the
twinkling of an eye, at the last trumpet; for the
trumpet shall sound, and the dead shall be raised
incorruptible, and *we* shall be changed. For this
corruptible *must* put on incorruption, and this
mortal must put on immortality.' This will be a

great, and an instantaneous change of corruptible
for incorruption, and of mortal for immortality, of
which we can now have no adequate conception.
When this great and mighty change shall take
place, then shall be the destruction of temporal
or bodily clay : see ver. 54 :—'So when this corruption shall have put on incorruption, then shall
be brought to pass the saying that is written,
Death is swallowed up in victory.' The glorious
truths that will also be brought to pass, in connexion with this saying, 'Death is swallowed up in
victory,' we have recorded in the prophecy of
Isaiah, chap. xxv. ver. 6—8 : 'And in this moun-
tain, shall the Lord of hosts make unto all people
a feast of fat things, a feast of wines on the lees ;
of fat things full of marrow, of wines. on the lees
well refined. And he will destroy in this moun-
tain, the face of the covering cast over all people,
and the vail that is spread over all nations. He
will swallow up death in victory; and the Lord
God will wipe away tears from off all faces; and
the rebuke of his people shall he take away from
off all the earth ; for the Lord hath spoken it.'
So we see that this glorious feast, that shall be
made unto *all people*, is to be fulfilled, according
to the sense of the apostle, when this mortal shall
have put on immortality, and this corruptible is
clothed with incorruption. In confirmation of this
glorious truth, the revelator hath said—Rev. xxi.
3, 4—'Behold, the tabernacle of God is (or shall
be) with men, and he will dwell with them, and
they shall be his people, and God himself shall be
with them, and be their God. And God shall
wipe away all tears from their eyes ; and there

shall be no more *death*, neither sorrow nor crying, neither shall there be any more pain; for the former things are passed away.'

The apostle then tells us what creates the terrors of a dying scene, even sin against the laws of God. See ver. 56 :—'The sting of death is sin ; and the strength of sin is the law.' Then follow the words of the text :—'But thanks be to God, which giveth us the victory through our Lord Jesus Christ.'

II. As a practical improvement of the text, we may consider, 1st, What death is, with some of its accidents and consequences. 2d, How Christ hath mitigated its terrors, and given us the victory over it—and take notice of our obligations to him for so inestimable a favor.

1st, Death, as it respects only our body, is the extinction of our mere animal life, which is common to man, beasts, birds, creeping things, and all animated nature, and is generally attended with great and exquisite pain and distress. This is evident, (except when the cause is too sudden to be felt,) from apparent circumstances, and also, as it is reasonable to suppose, upon so great an effect as will cause all the vital powers, and every coarser and finer nerve of the human frame, to cease to operate.

Our bodies, at death, are left with our friends, to be interred in the cold and silent earth, and to crumble and moulder back to their primordinal dust. ' Then shall the dust return to the earth as it was ; and the spirit shall return unto God who gave it.'

At death, we close our eyes on all this transitory

world, and the changing scenes of things. We bid adieu, for a longer or a shorter time, as God shall please, to kindred, friends, and neighbors—to all the joys, all the sorrows, and all the trifles of time and sense.

Death transmits our souls into the presence of our Maker, and into a new and unexperienced scene of things, of which we can now form but very imperfect ideas.

But as we are moral and accountable beings, so it is the scriptural idea, that death is succeeded by our actual appearance in the more immediate and sensible presence of God and the Lamb, of whom we shall receive such sentence and appointment as will be consistent for a Being of infinite goodness, justice, mercy, love, and truth, to give.

Of the process of this personal interview and examination before God and the Lamb, which taketh away the sin of the world, we are greatly unacquainted; though, as a certain consequence of death, we have the utmost reason to expect it. Here, 'we know in part and we prophesy in part; but, when that which is perfect is come, then that which is in part shall be done away.' 'Therefore, judge nothing before the time, until the Lord come, who both will bring to light the hidden things of darkness, and will make manifest the counsels of the heart; and then shall every man have praise of God,' 1 Cor. xiii. 9, 10:—iv. 5.

After this important interview with our Maker, we shall enter into that society, and upon the employments and enjoyments—or into that state of suffering and punishment inseparably connected with sin,* to which we shall be destined by infinite wisdom and goodness.

2d, How Christ hath mitigated the terrors of death, and given us the victory over it, with our obligations to him for so inestimable a favor.

After the apostle had plainly told us what created the terrors of death, even sin, and what gave sin its terrific efficacy, even the law of God, he devoutly thanks God that he hath given Christians the victory over death, i. e., had removed its terrors, and unclothed it of its dreadful appearance and frightful garb, &c., through Jesus Christ.

Hence, by the help of our context, we may discover what Christ hath done to free us from the dread and terror of a dying hour.

1st, 'He hath died for our sins.'

Though we are sinners, we are sure of pardon, peace, aud reconciliation with God, through the merits of the Savior; for Christ came not to continue us *in* our sins, but to save us *from* our sins. 'For he shall save his people from their sins.' Reason dictates that this reflection must greatly mitigate the terror of death, and administer

---

* The reader will here notice, that Mr. Foster held to the doctrine of future punishment, though he believed in the final restoration of all rational intelligences to holiness snd happiness. These are his words :—' I frankly declare to you, that I feel myself disposed to extend the divinely-benevolent design of gospel grace and mercy, in such a manner as to include all the children of Adam. Nor can I possibly understand any definitions of the divine attributes, or interpretations of the declarations of the gospel itself, upon any other supposition of the extent of gospel grace and mercy. For this theory of the divine attributes and moral government, and extent of gospel grace and mercy, I am willing to write, to preach, and to converse, so long as I live, and shall be able to use my pen and tongue.' See Foster's Examination, page 289.

unspeakable comfort and consolation to the dying Christian.

2d, We have hope through Christ of a resurrection and a future life.

'If in this life only we have hope in Christ, we are of all men the most miserable.' But glory to God for his rich and sovereign grace, we are not left to temporary hopes from Christ. 'For as in Adam all die, even so in Christ shall all be made alive.' The effects of divine grace shall be as extensive as those of Adam's sin. 'For, where sin hath abounded, grace doth much more abound.'

When the dying Christian reflects, that what he now sows in corruption shall be raised in incorruption—what he sows in dishonor shall be raised in glory—what he sows in weakness shall be raised in power—what he sows a natural body shall be raised a spiritual body—with what divine consolation and glorious hope may he lay his body down to sleep in the dust, till God shall call it to celestial life!

Immortality, which was but conjectural by the wisest pagan philosophers, is clearly preached by the gospel, and demonstrated by the resurrection of Christ.

What returns of grateful praise and sincere obedience are due to God, who hath given us the victory over death, by the clear and certain hope of a blessed immortality through Jesus Christ!

3d, All needful and divine assistance and support, in a dying hour, may the Christian hope for, through Jesus Christ.

Our flesh is so weak, our natural faculties so frail and feeble, that after all the glorious hopes of peace and pardon through the blood of the ever-

8 †

lasting covenant, and of a resurrection to life and immortality, when death shall approach, we shall need the rod and staff of God for our support. This also we may hope for, since God hath assured us that he will never leave us nor forsake us.

IMPROVEMENT BY USUAL ADDRESSES.

I. To the children, and other surviving relatives of the deceased:—

You, my respected friends, are now called to attend the interment of the last remains of a kind and tender parent, whose presence, comfort, and assistance, you have long enjoyed.

This is, on many accounts, an affecting, solemn scene. She was an head of one of the earliest families who first settled this town. Though she never was captivated, nor received any personal injury from the savages, yet she endured many hardships and severe sufferings, on account of the injuries done to her connexions and friends, by the natives. A kind and indulgent husband, father of the children present, was presented to her a ghastly corpse, a victim of savage barbarity! O, the heart-aching pangs your mother then endured! She also suffered on account of the captivity of three of her children—of two of them for the long and painful term of three years and a few months. But, through the goodness of God, they were all returned to her joyful and grateful embraces again, and two of them are now alive, and attending on this solemn occasion.

She was born April 24th, 1710, and died May 5th, 1797, having just entered her 88th year.

A numerous posterity hath descended from her,

and, by her blood or affinity, she was connected
with a great part of the families in this town.
She left, at her death, two hundred and twenty-
seven lineal descendants.

And permit me to add, that, as your dear
departed mother was an early settler in this town,
she must have gone through a variety of troublesome scenes—experienced much of the goodness
of God, and many adverse providences. She hath
been a kind, indulgent parent, an obliging neighbor, a faithful friend, specially kind and useful
in times of sickness and distress, particularly in
the infant days of this settlement.

I am averse to the general practice of giving
characters in funeral avocations, or of being very
positive of the immediate happy state of departed
friends. But we have reason to hope, that the
goodness and mercy of God, in Christ Jesus, will
admit to eternal rest and peace, a friend who
hath seen and enjoyed, done and suffered, so much
as your departed mother hath.

You will do well to attend to her good advices,
and follow her good examples. Love God, and
Christ, and religion. Remember that nothing
but real religion can give you substantial comfort
when you come to die.

Remember that Christ hath conquered death,
and disarmed him of his terrors; so that all those
who believe in, and obey him, have nothing to fear
from that source.

Look now, my respected friends, into the grave;
it is the house appointed for you—for us all. Improve this providence to the glory of God, and let
it awaken your attention to the things of eternal
peace.

Be patient, submissive, resigned to God, and learn obedience by the things you suffer. May God be present with, assist and bless you, my dear friends, and sanctify this providence to you, for your eternal good.

2d, A few words to the whole congregation will close the subject.

You, my respected audience, are called to attend to the funeral solemnities of an aged neighbor, acquaintance, and friend—one of the first inhabitants of this town—who saw it in its infancy—in its maturer years, and in its present state.

Many of you, my aged fathers and mothers, are far advanced in life, and must quickly follow this aged mother in Israel, whose remains we this day inter. Many reflections will no doubt enter your minds on this occasion, but none can be more solemn, or more important, than this, that you must quickly die. Reflect that it is God's design, in this providence, to admonish, and do you good. It is a call to you:—'Be ye also ready.'

Remember, my fellow-travellers, bound with me to a vast eternity, and improve the gladsome idea, that God hath given us the victory over death, through our Lord Jesus Christ, to whom be glory for ever. Amen,

NAMES OF PERSONS KILLED IN CHARLESTOWN, NO. 4,
AND TIME WHEN—BY THE INDIANS.

Seth Putnam, May 2, 1748.—Samuel Farnsworth, Joseph Allen, Peter Perin, Aaron Lyon, Joseph Massey, May 24, 1746.—Jedediah Winchel June or July, 1746. —— Phips, August 3, 1746. —Isaac Goodale, Nathaniel Gould, October, 1747.—Obadiah Sartwell, June, 1749·—Lieut. Moses Willard, June 18, 1756.—Asahel Shebbins, August, 1748.—Josiah Kellogg, 1759.

———

NUMBER TAKEN PRISONERS BY THE INDIANS, FROM
CHARLESTOWN, NO. 4.

Capt. John Spafford, Isaac Parker, Stephen Farnsworth, April 19, 1746. —— Anderson, October, 1747.—Enos Stevens, June 17, 1749.— James Johnson, Susanna Johnson, Sylvanus Johnson, Susan Johnson, Polly Johnson, Miriam Willard, Peter Labarree, Ebenezer Farnsworth, August 29, 1754.—Sampson Colefax, David Farnsworth, Thomas Robins, Asa Spafford, May, 1756.—Mrs. Robins, Isaac Parker, David Hill, August, 1758.—Joseph Willard, wife and five children, June 7, 1760.

Albany, May 5, 1755.

MRS. JOHNSON:—I received yours of the 6th April, with one for your husband; it seems you are concerned whether or no he got safe here; it seems, also, by yours, that you mention to have received a letter from me, and none from your husband. When he left Albany to go to New England, he left me a letter for you, to be forwarded the first opportunity, which I did with that you received from me. I have expected your husband this three months past, to come and fetch you and your family. Since he left Albany, I never received a line from him, and the occasion of the delay I cannot conceive, without it is the difficulty to procure silver money. Keep good heart; I hope you will soon see your husband, is the wish from your humble servant,

JOHN W. LYDIUS.

FROM COL. CUYLER TO MR. JAMES JOHNSON.

Albany, June 17, 1755.

SIR:—I have received yours of the 7th and 8th instant, and have noted the contents. I really do not understand what you write me for in the first place; you say that my bills were not accepted—at the same time I find, by your draught on me, that you have received on my account 2300 livres, from Mr. La Corne St. Luc. I now send to him 438 dollars, for the payment of your draught. I am sorry that Mr. Rine de Cauogne has not accepted of my bills, for several reasons.

I have now desired La Corne St. Luc to let you have 700 livres, besides the 2300 which you have already received. I am, sir, your humble servant,

CORNELIUS CUYLER.

FROM MR. JOHNSON TO MISS MIRIAM WILLARD.

Quebec, April 16, 1756.

LOVING SISTER :—After our love to you, these are to inform you, that we are all well at present, as I hope these will find you and our little daughter, and all other friends at Montreal. I have written to you once before now, and we have had no answer, so that we do not know what your circumstances are, only that the general was so good as to let us know that you and Susanna were well. I would have you go to the general, and beg the favor to come down here to live with us; for I have written to the general, and begged the same favor. I would have you spare no pains, for, if you meet with any misfortunes, it will contribute very much to your parents' sorrow, as well as to ours. So I would not have you discouraged, or harbor any thoughts of staying in this country; for I do not doubt but we shall go home this summer; for I have desired the general to send home those of us that are paid for, and will stay in the country till there is a change of prisoners. And if you cannot come down, beg leave of the general to let you write to us; let us know what your circumstances are. Give my services to Mr. Du-

9

Quesne and madam, and to Susanna's mothers.—
We remain your loving brother and sister,

JAMES AND SUSANNA JOHNSON.

FROM MISS MIRIAM WILLARD TO MR. JOHNSON.

Written at Montreal, July or August, 1756.

LOVING BROTHER AND SISTER :—Having received yours of the 5th July, it being the second, though
you have sent four, wherein you give me to understand that my sister is not well, and that you
would have me come down—for which I have
asked the liberty of the general; he does not see
fit to let me come, unless I would go to prison,
and I think I am better off here than that comes
to ; therefore I take this opportunity to inform you
of my health at this time, and of Susanna, and all
the rest of the prisoners here, (and my love is
folded up in their lives,) with our friends that we
were taken with, to you and to all friends there.
Susanna has had the smallpox, and is prodigiously
marked. I would not have you be concerned
about my staying here, for the longer I stay the
more anxious desires I have to go bome.

MIRIAM WILLARD.

P. S. I hear, by Mr. Josiah Foster, of Winchester, who was taken on the 7th of June, with his
family, that our friends at No. 4 were all well,
and our brother James was returning from the
eastward.—No more at present. I shall subscribe
myself, in haste, your loving sister, M. W.

FROM MR. JOSIAH FOSTER, TO MR. JOHNSON.

Montreal, May 16, 1757.

SIR :—After my respects to you, your wife and sister, hoping you are in health, as we are at present, blessed be God for it. The 5th day of this present month, the Mowhawks brought in prisoners from No. 4, Mr. David Farnsworth, Sampson Colefax, Deacon Adams, Asa Spafford, and George Robins, which gives us the sorrowful news of the death of your father Willard, who was killed by the Indians last summer, a little way from the fort. Your brother Moses was stabbed in the thigh with a spear. This is all the mischief that has been done, except the Indians burnt the mills. Mr. Labarree has made his escape from Montreal, and has gone for the English fort. I should be glad to write you a fuller account of things, but it is very difficult to write. I should be glad you would write to me, to let me know how you are. So I remain your friend,

JOSIAH FOSTER.

FROM MRS. BISSON, TO MRS. JOHNSON, AFTER HER RETURN.

Quebec, Sept. 15, 1757.

MADAM :—It is with all possible pleasure, I do myself the pleasure to write, and to let you know the dulness I feel since your departure. One would not imagine it, considering the little time I had the happiness to be acquainted with you. I wish I had it in my power to convince you of the truth of it, but the distance hinders us ; you will know from your husband, how I have done all I could, to see he had done for him all the little services in my power. I pray you would salute Miss Miriam in my name, and tell her I wish her a pretty little husband at her return, worthy her merit. Embrace also your two little misses; my daughter, Mary Ann, assures you of her respects, and salutes kindly Miss Miriam and the two little misses. I beg you to enquire after my son, who, I believe is taken, because he is so long before he comes home. His name is James Bisson, son of James Bisson and Hubelle Badeau. I pray you again, that in case you find him, to do him what service you can, and to take care of him. I shall be everlastingly obliged to you for it. I conclude by assuring you, that I shall all my life be, madam, one of your greatest friends, and your humble servant,　　　　　　THE WIDOW BISSON.

Our neighbor, Miss Mary Ann Deforme, assures you of her respects, and salutes Miss Miriam and the two little misses. Miss Sinette and Tenesa Voyer assure you of their respects, and also Miss Mary Ann and the two misses. Adieu, Madam Johnson. I wish you health and much joy upon Mr. Johnson's return, who is to depart from hence immediately.

PASSPORT—BY GEN. MONCHTON.

Halifax, Oct. 19, 1757.

The bearer, Mr. James Johnson, is at liberty to take his passage on board any vessel bound to the continent.　　　　ROBERT MONCHTON.

FROM MR. JOHNSON. TO MRS. JOHNSON.

Fort Edward, June 22, 1758.
MY DEAR :—This day I have had the sorrowful
news of the loss of my dear child. May God
sanctify this and all other of his afflictive dispensations to us. I am in good health at present, blessed
be God for it, hoping this will find you and the
rest of my dear children in like manner. We are
to march to-morrow to the lake. I have nothing
remarkable to tell you. I am in haste, so I remain your most loving husband,
JAMES JOHNSON.

CAPTAIN JOHNSON'S COMMISSION.

Province of the Massachusetts Bay.

THOMAS POWNALL, Esq., Captain General and
Governor in Chief, in and over his Ma-
jesty's Province of the Massachusetts
L. S. Bay, in New England, and Vice Admiral
of the same, &c., to JAMES JOHNSON,
Esq., *Greeting :—*

By Virtue of the Power and Authority in and
by His Majesty's Royal Commission to me granted
to be Captain General, &c., over this His Majesty's Province of the Massachusetts Bay aforesaid,
I do by these Presents (reposing especial Trust
and Confidence in your Loyalty, Courage and
good Conduct) Constitute and Appoint You the
said James Johnson to be Captain of a Company
in the Battallion of Light Infantry to be formed

out of the Forces now raised by me for a general
Invasion of Canada, commanded by Col. Oliver
Partridge.

You are therfore carfully and diligently to
discharge the Duty of a Captain in leading, ordering and exercising said company in Arms, both
inferior Officers and Soldiers, and to keep them
in good Order and Discipline, and they are hereby
commanded to obey you as their Captain; and
you are yourself to observe and follow such Orders
and Instructions, as you shall from time to time
receive from the General and Commander in
Chief of His Majesty's Forces in North America,
your Colonel or any other your superior Officer
according to the Rules and Discipline of War in
pursuance of the Trust hereby reposed in You.

*Given under my Hand and Seal at Arms at
Boston, the thirtieth Day of March, in the
thirty-first Year of the Reign of His Majesty
King George the Second, Anno Domini, 1758.*
T. Pownall.

By His Excellency's Command.
A. Oliver, *Secretary.*

THE END.

Made in the USA
Las Vegas, NV
30 August 2021